THE ULTIMATE GUIDE TO AFFILIATE MARKETING

HOW TO PASSIVE INCOME ONLINE

By Alexander J. Kelley

The Ultimate Guide to Affiliate Marketing: How to Make Passive Income Online

Copyright © 2023 by Alexander J. Kelley

All rights reserved.

No portion of this book may be reproduced in any form without written permission from the publisher or author, except as permitted by U.S. copyright law.

This publication is designed to provide accurate and authoritative information regarding the subject matter covered. It is sold with the understanding that neither the author nor the publisher is engaged in rendering legal, investment, accounting, or other professional services. While the publisher and author have used their best efforts in preparing this book, they make no representations or warranties with respect to the accuracy or completeness of the contents of this book and specifically disclaim any implied warranties of merchantability or fitness for a particular purpose. No warranty may be created or extended by sales representatives or written sales materials. The advice and strategies contained herein may not be suitable for your situation. You should consult with a professional when appropriate. Neither the publisher nor the author shall be liable for any loss of profit or any other commercial damages, including but not limited to special, incidental, consequential, personal, or other damages.

Book Cover by Alexander J. Kelley

First Edition 2023

www.alexanderkelley.com

To my dad, James.
Thank you for instilling out of the box thinking.
I love you.

Table of Contents

Introduction 7
   Welcome! Here's What You Can Expect 8

Chapter 1: The World of Affiliate Marketing 9
   What is Affiliate Marketing? 10
   Why Affiliate Marketing is a Great Way to Make Passive Income 12
   How to Get Started with Affiliate Marketing 14

Chapter 2: Choosing Your Niche 18
   Understanding Niches & Why They Are Important 19
   How to Choose the Right Niche for You 21
   Evaluating Profitability & Competition in Your Niche 24

Chapter 3: Building Your Online Presence 26
   Setting Up Your Website or Blog 27
   Creating Quality Content for your Site 29
   Building Your Email List and Social Media Presence 32

Chapter 4: Finding the Right Affiliate Programs 34
   How to Find the Best Affiliate Programs 35
   Evaluating Affiliate Programs for Quality and Profitability 39
   Choosing the Right Affiliate Programs for Your Niche 42

Chapter 5: Understanding Affiliate Marketing Terminology 44
   Understanding Affiliate Marketing Terms 45
   How Affiliate Networks Work 48
   Understanding Commission Structures 50

Chapter 6: Creating Great Content to Promote Affiliate Products 52
   How to Create High-Quality Content 53
   Using Keywords and SEO to Drive Traffic to Your Site 55
   How to Write Reviews and Promote Products Effectively 58

Chapter 7: Maximizing Your Affiliate Earnings 61
   Tips and Strategies for Increasing Your Affiliate Earnings 62
   Leveraging Social Media and Other Channels to Promote Affiliate Products 64
   Building Relationships with Your Audience and Affiliate Partners 67

Chapter 8: Creating a Sales Funnel for Affiliate Marketing 70
   Understanding Sales Funnels and How They Work 71
   Creating Your Own Sales Funnel for Affiliate Marketing 74
   Maximizing Your Profits with a Sales Funnel 77

Chapter 9: Using Paid Advertising to Promote Affiliate Products 80
   Understanding Paid Advertising 81
   Choosing the Right Advertising Channels 84
   Creating Effective Ads for Affiliate Marketing 87

Chapter 10: Scaling Your Affiliate Marketing Business 90
   How to Grow Your Affiliate Marketing Business 91
   Outsourcing and Automating Tasks for Efficiency 94
   Building Your Own Affiliate Program 96

Chapter 11: Overcoming Challenges in Affiliate Marketing 98
   Common Challenges Faced by Affiliate Marketers 99
   How to Overcome These Challenges & Succeed in Affiliate Marketing .101
   Tips and Strategies for Long-Term Success 103

Chapter 12: Staying Informed of the Latest Affiliate Marketing Trends ... 105
   Understanding the Latest Affiliate Marketing Trends 106
   Staying Ahead of the Curve in Affiliate Marketing 108
   Using New Strategies and Technologies to Improve Your Affiliate Marketing 110

Chapter 13: Legal & Ethical Considerations in Affiliate Marketing 112
   Understanding the Legal and Ethical Issues in Affiliate Marketing 113
   Complying with FTC Regulations 115

    Protecting Your Reputation and Your Audience 118

Chapter 14: Case Studies and Success Stories in Affiliate Marketing 120

    Learning from Other Successful Affiliate Marketers 121

    Case Studies and Success Stories in Affiliate Marketing 127

    What You Can Learn from Their Strategies and Techniques 130

Chapter 15: The Next Steps Are Yours 132

    Key Takeaways from this Book 133

    Putting Knowledge into Practice 135

Conclusion 137

    Moving Forward with Your Affiliate Marketing Business 138

    A Message from The Author 140

Introduction

Introduction

Welcome! Here's What You Can Expect

Welcome to "The Ultimate Guide to Affiliate Marketing: How to Make Passive Income Online"! This book is designed to be a comprehensive resource for anyone who wants to learn about affiliate marketing and how to make money online. Whether you're a complete novice to affiliate marketing or an experienced marketer looking to improve your skills, this book has something for everyone.

Throughout the book, you can expect to learn about the fundamentals of affiliate marketing, including how it works, the different types of affiliate programs available, and how to choose the right affiliate products to promote. You'll also learn about the importance of building a strong online presence and the various marketing strategies you can use to promote affiliate products effectively.

This book is designed to be a practical guide, with step-by-step instructions, case studies, and real-world examples to help you apply the concepts and techniques to your own affiliate marketing campaigns. You'll also learn about the tools and resources available to help you succeed in affiliate marketing, including affiliate networks, analytics tools, and email marketing platforms.

Whether you're looking to start a side hustle or build a full-time business, this book will provide you with the knowledge and skills you need to succeed in affiliate marketing and make passive income online. So, sit back, relax, and get ready to learn everything you need to know to become a successful affiliate marketer!

Chapter 1: The World of Affiliate Marketing

Chapter 1

What is Affiliate Marketing?

Affiliate marketing is a type of online marketing in which an affiliate promotes a product or service on behalf of a business or advertiser. The affiliate is rewarded for their efforts with a commission for each sale, click or lead generated through their unique affiliate link.

The concept of affiliate marketing is based on the traditional commission-based sales model, where salespeople are compensated for their efforts in promoting and selling a product. However, with affiliate marketing, anyone can become a salesperson and earn money by promoting products or services that they believe in.

Affiliate marketing has become increasingly popular in recent years due to the rise of e-commerce and the increasing number of businesses operating online. Affiliate marketing allows businesses to reach a wider audience and increase their sales without having to invest in expensive advertising campaigns. For affiliates, it offers an opportunity to earn money from home or anywhere they have an internet connection, making it an attractive source of passive income.

The process of affiliate marketing typically involves the following steps:

1. Affiliate selection: The affiliate selects a product or service they wish to promote and applies to join the affiliate program.
2. Approval: The advertiser reviews the affiliate application and approves or denies the affiliate's request to join their program.
3. Promotion: The affiliate promotes the product or service to their audience using various marketing techniques, including blog posts, social media, email marketing, and paid advertising.
4. Sales tracking: When a customer clicks on the affiliate link and makes a purchase, the sale is tracked using a unique affiliate code or link.
5. Commission payment: The affiliate is paid a commission for each sale, click, or lead generated through their unique affiliate link, typically monthly.

Affiliate marketing can be a lucrative source of income for those who are willing to put in the time and effort to promote products or services to their audience. It can also be an effective way for businesses to expand their reach and increase their sales without investing in costly advertising campaigns.

Chapter 1

Why Affiliate Marketing is a Great Way to Make Passive Income

Affiliate marketing is one of the best ways to make passive income online. Unlike traditional forms of employment, affiliate marketing allows you to earn money while you sleep, as your affiliate links continue to generate sales and leads even when you're not actively promoting them. Here are some of the reasons why affiliate marketing is such a great way to make passive income:

1. Low startup costs: Affiliate marketing has very low startup costs, making it accessible to anyone who wants to start an online business. All you need is a computer and an internet connection, and you can start promoting affiliate products right away.
2. No inventory or shipping: As an affiliate, you don't need to worry about inventory or shipping. The product owner takes care of all of that, leaving you free to focus on promoting the product and earning commissions.
3. Wide variety of products: There are millions of products and services available for affiliate marketing, so you're sure to find something that aligns with your interests and values. This means you can promote products you believe in and feel good about the sales you generate.
4. Flexibility: Affiliate marketing allows you to work from anywhere and on your own schedule. You can choose which products to promote, how to promote them, and when to promote them, giving you the freedom to create a business that works for you.
5. High earning potential: With the right strategies and techniques, affiliate marketing can be a highly lucrative source of passive income. The commission rates for affiliate products vary, but many pay out 50% or more of the sale price, meaning you can earn a significant income with just a few sales.

6. Scalability: Affiliate marketing is scalable, meaning you can grow your income over time by promoting more products and reaching a larger audience. You can also outsource some of the tasks involved in affiliate marketing, such as content creation and social media management, allowing you to focus on the areas where you excel.
7. Low risk: Affiliate marketing is a low-risk business model because you don't need to invest a lot of money upfront. If a product doesn't sell well, you can simply stop promoting it and move on to something else. This makes affiliate marketing an ideal option for those who are risk-averse or who are just starting out in online business.

In summary, affiliate marketing is a fantastic way to make passive income online. With low startup costs, no inventory or shipping concerns, a wide variety of products to choose from, flexibility, high earning potential, scalability, and low risk, it's no wonder that affiliate marketing has become so popular in recent years.

Chapter 1

How to Get Started with Affiliate Marketing

If you're interested in making passive income through affiliate marketing, the good news is that it's relatively easy to get started. Here are the steps you need to follow to begin your journey as an affiliate marketer:

Step 1: Choose a niche.

The first step in starting with affiliate marketing is to choose a niche or topic that you are interested in and passionate about. This will help you create content that resonates with your audience and makes it easier to promote affiliate products that align with your niche.

Step 2: Select affiliate programs.

Once you have chosen your niche, the next step is to select the affiliate programs you want to join. Start by researching reputable affiliate programs that offer products or services that are relevant to your niche. Some popular affiliate programs include Amazon Associates, ClickBank, and Share Sale. Here is a complete list of the most popular affiliate marketing programs and networks that you might want to consider:

1. Amazon Associates: Amazon's affiliate program is one of the most popular and widely used programs in the industry, offering commissions for promoting products across the Amazon platform.
2. ClickBank: ClickBank is a popular affiliate network that specializes in digital products like eBooks, courses, and software.
3. ShareASale: ShareASale is an affiliate network that offers a wide range of products to promote across various niches, including fashion, home and garden, and health and wellness.
4. Commission Junction: Commission Junction is a popular affiliate network that offers a wide range of products and services to promote across various niches.
5. Rakuten Marketing: Rakuten Marketing is an affiliate network that offers a wide range of products to promote across various niches, including fashion, electronics, and travel.

6. eBay Partner Network: eBay Partner Network is eBay's affiliate program that offers commissions for promoting products across the eBay platform.
7. Shopify Affiliate Program: Shopify's affiliate program offers commissions for promoting their ecommerce platform and related services.
8. ClickFunnels Affiliate Program: ClickFunnels is a popular funnel-building software that offers an affiliate program for promoting their product.
9. Bluehost Affiliate Program: Bluehost is a popular web hosting provider that offers an affiliate program for promoting their hosting services.
10. MaxBounty: MaxBounty is an affiliate network that specializes in CPA (cost per action) offers, such as free trials and sign-ups.

Step 3: Build a platform.

To promote affiliate products, you need to have a platform where you can reach your target audience. This could be a website, blog, or social media account. You can also use email marketing to reach out to your audience. Whichever medium you choose, you are some of the more popular resources to help you get started:

1. WordPress: WordPress is a popular and user-friendly content management system that allows you to build a website or blog. With its easy-to-use interface and customizable features, it's a great platform for creating and sharing content with your target audience.
2. Wix: Wix is a website builder that allows you to create a website using drag-and-drop tools. It's a user-friendly platform that offers a range of features to help you build a website quickly and easily.
3. Squarespace: Squarespace is a website builder that offers a range of templates and features to help you build a professional-looking website. It's a great option for those who want a visually stunning website without having to know how to code.
4. Social Media Platforms: Social media platforms like Facebook, Twitter, Instagram, LinkedIn, and Pinterest are great tools for building a platform to reach your target audience. By sharing

content and engaging with your audience on these platforms, you can build a loyal following and drive traffic to your website or blog.
5. Email Marketing Platforms: Email marketing platforms like Mailchimp, ConvertKit, and Aweber allow you to create and send newsletters and promotional emails to your subscribers. This is a great way to stay in touch with your audience and keep them engaged with your content.
6. Online Communities: Online communities like Reddit, Quora, and Facebook Groups are great platforms for building relationships with your target audience. By joining and engaging in these communities, you can establish yourself as an expert in your niche and build a loyal following.
7. Podcasts and Videos: Podcasts and videos are great platforms for reaching your target audience with engaging content. Platforms like YouTube and iTunes allow you to publish and promote your content to a wide audience.

Step 4: Create content.

Once you have your platform set up, the next step is to create content that provides value to your audience. This could include blog posts, videos, podcasts, or social media posts. Your content should be informative, engaging, and relevant to your niche.

Step 5: Promote affiliate products.

Once you have created content, you can begin promoting affiliate products. This can be done through product reviews, tutorials, or by including affiliate links in your content. Make sure to disclose your affiliate relationship with your audience to maintain transparency and build trust.

Step 6: Track your results.

It's important to track your results to see what is working and what is not. Use analytics tools to measure the performance of your content and track the number of clicks, leads, and sales generated through your affiliate links. This will help you optimize your campaigns for better results.

Step 7: Rinse and repeat.

As you start to see results, continue to create content, promote affiliate products, and track your results. Over time, you can refine your strategy and build a profitable affiliate marketing business.

Getting started with affiliate marketing requires some effort and dedication, but it can be a great way to make passive income online. By choosing a niche you're passionate about, joining reputable affiliate programs, creating valuable content, and promoting affiliate products, you can build a successful affiliate marketing business that generates passive income for years to come.

Chapter 2: Choosing Your Niche

Chapter 2

Understanding Niches & Why They Are Important

In the world of affiliate marketing, understanding niches is essential to building a successful business and making passive income. A niche is a specific area of focus or expertise, such as health and wellness, personal finance, or home improvement. By choosing a niche, you can target a specific audience and create content that is tailored to their needs and interests. In this chapter, we will explore the importance of understanding niches and how they can help you achieve your affiliate marketing goals.

One of the primary reasons that niches are important in affiliate marketing is that they allow you to stand out from the competition. By focusing on a specific niche, you can become an expert in that area and offer valuable insights and recommendations to your audience. This can help you build trust and establish yourself as a go-to resource for information and products related to your niche.

Another reason why niches are important is that they help you identify your target audience. When you know who your audience is, you can create content that speaks directly to their needs and interests. This can help you attract and retain a loyal following and drive more traffic and sales to your affiliate offers.

Additionally, focusing on a specific niche can help you narrow down your competition. While there may be many affiliates promoting products in broad categories like health or finance, by choosing a sub-niche, you can reduce the competition and increase your chances of success.

When choosing a niche, it's important to consider factors like market demand, profitability, and competition. You want to choose a niche that has a large enough audience to support your business, but not so much competition that it's difficult to stand out.

Once you've chosen your niche, it's important to conduct thorough research and stay current with industry trends and developments. This can help you create content that is relevant and valuable to your audience and identify new opportunities for growth and revenue.

Another important aspect of understanding niches is recognizing that they can change over time. As your business grows and evolves, you may find that your niche needs to be adjusted or expanded to better serve your audience. By staying flexible and open to change, you can ensure that your business stays relevant and successful in the long term.

In conclusion, understanding niches is essential to building a successful affiliate marketing business. By choosing a niche, you can target a specific audience, stand out from the competition, and establish yourself as an expert in your area of focus. Remember to research your niche thoroughly, stay up to date with industry trends, and remain flexible and adaptable as your business grows and evolves. By following these tips, you can create a thriving affiliate marketing business that generates passive income and helps you achieve your goals.

Chapter 2

How to Choose the Right Niche for You

Choosing the right niche is critical when it comes to affiliate marketing success. Your niche will determine the audience you target, the products you promote, and ultimately, the amount of revenue you can generate. In this chapter, we'll explore some key factors to consider when choosing the right niche for you.

The first step in choosing a niche is to consider your interests and passions. This is important because building a successful affiliate marketing business takes time, effort, and dedication. Choosing a niche that you're passionate about will make the work more enjoyable and sustainable in the long run.

Once you have a list of potential niches, the next step is to evaluate the market demand. You want to choose a niche that has a large enough audience to support your business. Conduct market research to determine the size of the market and the potential for growth. You can use tools like Google Trends, Amazon Bestsellers, and keyword research tools to help you evaluate market demand.

Profitability is another important factor to consider when choosing a niche. You want to choose a niche that has a high potential for profitability. This means evaluating the commission rates and the average order value for products in your niche. Look for niches where customers are willing to spend money, and where you can earn a decent commission.

Competition is another important factor to consider when choosing a niche. Look for niches where the competition isn't too high. While some competition is healthy, too much can make it difficult to stand out and generate revenue. Use tools like SEMrush, Ahrefs, or Moz to research your potential competitors and evaluate their strengths and weaknesses.

Once you've evaluated your interests, market demand, profitability, and competition, it's time to narrow down your list of potential niches. Consider the potential for growth in each niche and choose one that aligns with your goals and interests. Remember, the niche you choose will impact the content you create and the products you promote, so choose wisely.

Once you've chosen your niche, it's time to conduct even more research. This includes identifying the key players in your niche, learning more about your target audience, and identifying the most popular products and services. You can use tools like BuzzSumo to research your niche and stay up to date with industry trends. Additional tools and resources include:

1. Affiliate marketing networks: These are platforms that connect affiliate marketers with merchants who are looking for affiliates to promote their products. By browsing through these networks, you can discover popular niches and the products that are currently in demand.
2. Online communities and forums: Joining online communities and forums related to your potential niche can provide valuable insights into what your audience is looking for and what products or services they're interested in.
3. Keyword research tools: Keyword research tools such as Google AdWords Keyword Planner or Ahrefs can help you identify the keywords that people are using to search for products in your niche. This can give you an idea of the potential demand for those products.
4. Social media platforms: Social media platforms such as Facebook, Twitter, and Instagram can be great resources for researching your potential niche. By following influencers and businesses in your niche, you can learn more about the products and services that are currently popular.
5. Google Trends: Google Trends can help you identify the popularity of certain keywords and topics over time. This can give you an idea of whether your potential niche is growing or declining in popularity.

It's also important to stay flexible and open to change. As your business grows and evolves, you may find that your niche needs to be adjusted or expanded to better serve your audience. By staying flexible and open to change, you can ensure that your business stays relevant and successful in the long term.

Choosing the right niche is critical to affiliate marketing success. Consider your interests, evaluate market demand and profitability, and evaluate your competition. Narrow down your list of potential niches, conduct thorough research, and stay flexible as your business grows and evolves. By following these tips, you can choose a niche that aligns with your goals and interests and create a thriving affiliate marketing business that generates passive income.

Chapter 2

Evaluating Profitability & Competition in Your Niche

Choosing the right niche for your affiliate marketing business is just the first step in building a successful passive income stream. Once you have identified a potential niche, it's crucial to evaluate its profitability and competition. This process will help you determine whether your chosen niche has the potential to generate the passive income you're looking for. By evaluating profitability and competition in your niche, you can make an informed decision about whether it's worth investing your time and resources into.

In this section, we'll guide you through the steps to evaluate profitability and competition in your niche, so you can choose a profitable niche that has the potential to generate passive income for you. Here's how you can evaluate profitability and competition in your niche:

1. Conduct market research: Start by conducting market research to determine the size of your potential audience and their buying habits. Look for data on the total addressable market size, target demographics, and customer behavior. This will give you a better idea of the potential profitability of your niche.
2. Analyze your competition: Research your competition to determine the level of competition in your niche. Look for competitors' websites, products, and pricing strategies. By understanding your competitors, you can determine whether there is room for you to enter the market and succeed.
3. Evaluate the profitability of products: Look for products in your niche that have high commissions and are in high demand. Evaluate the profit margins of these products and ensure that they are profitable enough to make it worth your time and effort to promote them.
4. Look for gaps in the market: Look for gaps in the market that you can fill. Are there products or services that are in high demand but not yet being offered by your competitors? If so, this could be an

opportunity for you to differentiate yourself and gain a competitive advantage.
5. Consider the long-term potential: Evaluate the long-term potential of your niche. Is it a niche that is likely to grow or shrink in the future? By considering the long-term potential of your niche, you can make an informed decision about whether it's worth investing your time and resources into.
6. Use keyword research tools: Use keyword research tools such as Google AdWords Keyword Planner or Ahrefs to identify the keywords that people are using to search for products in your niche. This can give you an idea of the potential demand for those products.
7. Look for affiliate programs: Look for affiliate programs in your niche that offer high commissions and have a good reputation. This can help you determine whether it's worth promoting products in your niche and which products are likely to be the most profitable.

By evaluating profitability and competition in your niche, you can make an informed decision about whether it's worth investing your time and resources into. Remember to conduct thorough market research, analyze your competition, evaluate the profitability of products, look for gaps in the market, consider the long-term potential, use keyword research tools, and look for reputable affiliate programs. With this information, you can choose a profitable niche that has the potential to generate passive income for you.

Chapter 3: Building Your Online Presence

Chapter 3

Setting Up Your Website or Blog

Congratulations on choosing your niche! Now, it's time to build your website or blog to promote your affiliate products. Your website or blog is the foundation of your affiliate marketing business, and it's crucial to get it right. In this section, we'll guide you through the steps to set up your website or blog, so you can start promoting your affiliate products and generating passive income.

1. Choose a domain name and hosting provider: Your domain name is the address of your website or blog, and your hosting provider is where your website or blog will be stored online. Choose a domain name that's relevant to your niche, easy to remember, and easy to spell. For hosting, we recommend using a reliable hosting provider that offers good speed and uptime.
2. Install a content management system (CMS): A CMS is a software that helps you manage the content on your website or blog. WordPress is the most popular CMS, and it's free and easy to use. Once you have chosen your hosting provider, you can install WordPress in just a few clicks.
3. Choose a theme: A theme is a design template that determines the look and feel of your website or blog. Choose a theme that's easy to navigate, visually appealing, and relevant to your niche. You can choose from thousands of free and paid themes in the WordPress theme directory.
4. Install essential plugins: Plugins are software that adds functionality to your website or blog. Some essential plugins for affiliate marketing include an SEO plugin (to optimize your website for search engines), a caching plugin (to improve website speed), and a social sharing plugin (to encourage social sharing of your content).
5. Create content: Once you have set up your website or blog, it's time to start creating content. Your content should be relevant to your niche, informative, and engaging. It's important to publish regular content to keep your audience engaged and to improve your website's search engine rankings.

6. Optimize your content for search engines: Search engine optimization (SEO) is the process of optimizing your website or blog to rank higher in search engine results pages (SERPs). SEO involves keyword research, optimizing your content with relevant keywords, and optimizing your website's structure and navigation.
7. Build an email list: An email list is a list of subscribers who have given you permission to email them. Building an email list is important for affiliate marketing because it allows you to build a relationship with your audience and promote your affiliate products directly to them.
8. Monetize your website or blog: There are several ways to monetize your website or blog, including affiliate marketing, advertising, and sponsored content. Affiliate marketing is the focus of this book, but it's important to consider other monetization options as well.

By following these steps, you can set up a website or blog that's optimized for affiliate marketing and start promoting your affiliate products to your audience. Remember, building a successful affiliate marketing business takes time and effort, but with the right approach, it's possible to generate a passive income stream that can change your life.

Chapter 3

Creating Quality Content for your Site

Creating quality content for your website is one of the most important aspects of running a successful affiliate marketing business. Your website's content is what will attract visitors, establish your authority in your niche, and ultimately drive traffic to the products and services you are promoting. In this section, we will discuss the key principles of creating high-quality content that will help you achieve your affiliate marketing goals.

First and foremost, it's important to understand your audience and their needs. You should create content that is specifically tailored to your target audience and speaks directly to their interests, pain points, and desires. This means conducting thorough research to understand your audience's preferences and motivations.

Once you have a clear understanding of your audience, it's time to start creating content that will capture their attention and keep them engaged. One of the most effective ways to do this is by providing value through your content. Whether it's through informative blog posts, in-depth product reviews, or engaging video content, your content should always aim to educate, inspire, or entertain your audience.

Another important principle of creating quality content is to ensure that it is visually appealing and easy to read. This means using a clean and easy-to-navigate website layout, incorporating high-quality images and videos, and using clear and concise language. Avoid cluttering your website with excessive ads or unnecessary elements that can distract from your content.

In addition to creating content that is valuable and visually appealing, it's also important to ensure that it is optimized for search engines. This means using relevant keywords and phrases throughout your content to help it rank higher in search results. However, it's important to avoid keyword stuffing or other tactics that can harm your search engine rankings and credibility.

Another important aspect of creating quality content is consistency. Regularly publishing fresh, relevant content is key to building and maintaining your audience. This means developing a content calendar and sticking to a regular publishing schedule. It's also important to keep your content up-to-date and relevant, regularly reviewing and updating older content as necessary.

Finally, it's important to make your content shareable and encourage social engagement. This means incorporating social media buttons and sharing options into your content, as well as actively engaging with your audience on social media platforms. By creating content that is valuable, visually appealing, optimized for search engines, consistent, and shareable, you can establish your authority in your niche and drive traffic to your affiliate products and services. Here are some of the more popular tools and resources that should come in handy:

1. Content management systems (CMS) such as WordPress, Drupal, and Joomla make it easy to create and publish content on your website. These platforms provide a range of templates, plugins, and add-ons to help you optimize your content for search engines and make it more visually appealing.
2. Keyword research tools like Google Keyword Planner, Ahrefs, and SEMrush can help you identify relevant keywords and phrases to include in your content. These tools provide valuable insights into search volume, competition, and related keywords, which can help you optimize your content for search engines and improve its relevance to your target audience.
3. Writing and editing tools like Grammarly and Hemingway can help you improve the quality of your writing by identifying spelling and grammar errors, suggesting sentence rewrites, and providing readability scores. These tools can help you create content that is more engaging and easier to read.
4. Design tools like Canva and Adobe Creative Suite can help you create high-quality images, graphics, and videos to accompany your content. These tools provide a range of templates, design elements, and editing tools to help you create professional-looking visuals for your website.

5. Social media scheduling and management tools like Hootsuite and Buffer can help you manage and promote your content on social media platforms. These tools allow you to schedule posts, track engagement, and monitor your social media presence from a single dashboard.

Creating quality content is essential to the success of your affiliate marketing website. By providing valuable information, engaging your audience, and optimizing your content for search engines, you can attract more visitors to your site and increase your chances of generating affiliate sales. Remember to focus on your niche, be consistent in your content creation, and leverage the right tools and resources to optimize your content for maximum impact. With time and effort, you can build a successful affiliate marketing website that generates passive income for years to come.

Chapter 3

Building Your Email List and Social Media Presence

As you build your affiliate marketing website and create quality content, it's essential to focus on building your email list and social media presence. These channels provide additional opportunities to engage with your audience and promote your affiliate products. In this section, we'll explore how to build your email list and social media presence effectively.

1. Building Your Email List: Your email list is a valuable asset for your affiliate marketing business. It allows you to reach out to your audience directly and promote your affiliate products. To build your email list, you can offer a lead magnet, such as a free e-book, guide, or checklist, in exchange for your visitors' email addresses. Place opt-in forms on your website to encourage your visitors to sign up for your email list.
2. Creating Effective Email Campaigns: Once you have built your email list, it's essential to create effective email campaigns that engage your audience and promote your affiliate products. Make sure your emails provide value to your subscribers, such as helpful tips or exclusive offers. You can also include product reviews or testimonials to showcase the benefits of the affiliate products you are promoting.
3. Leveraging Social Media: Social media provides another channel for promoting your affiliate products and engaging with your audience. Start by choosing the social media platforms that are most relevant to your niche and target audience. Share your content regularly and engage with your followers by responding to comments and messages. You can also run social media ads to reach a wider audience and drive traffic to your affiliate marketing website.
4. Creating Engaging Social Media Content: To be successful on social media, you need to create engaging content that resonates with your audience. Share helpful tips, inspiring quotes, and behind-the-scenes glimpses of your affiliate marketing journey. You can also use social

media to promote your content, such as blog posts or videos, and drive traffic to your website.
5. Building Relationships with Influencers: Influencer marketing can be a powerful way to promote your affiliate products and reach a wider audience. Look for influencers in your niche and build relationships with them by engaging with their content and reaching out to them directly. You can offer to collaborate on content or promotions to reach their audience and promote your affiliate products.

Building your email list and social media presence are essential to the success of your affiliate marketing business. Focus on providing value to your audience, engaging with them regularly, and leveraging the right tools and resources to build your email list and social media presence effectively. With time and effort, you can build a loyal following and generate passive income through your affiliate marketing website.

Chapter 4: Finding the Right Affiliate Programs

Chapter 4

How to Find the Best Affiliate Programs

Affiliate marketing is an excellent way to earn passive income by promoting other people's products and earning a commission for every sale made through your unique affiliate link. However, not all affiliate programs are created equal, and finding the best ones to promote can make a significant difference in your earnings. In this section, we will discuss how to find the best affiliate programs for your niche and audience.

One way to find affiliate programs is by searching for them on Google. You can search for terms like "[your niche] + affiliate program" or "[product name] + affiliate program" to find relevant programs. Another option is to use affiliate networks like Amazon Associates, ShareASale, and Commission Junction, which offer a wide range of affiliate programs in different niches.

When evaluating affiliate programs, it's important to consider the commission rate, the quality of the product or service, and the conversion rate. A high commission rate may seem appealing, but if the product is of poor quality or has a low conversion rate, you may not make many sales. On the other hand, promoting a high-quality product with a lower commission rate may result in more sales and ultimately more earnings.

It's also important to consider the affiliate program's terms and conditions. Some programs may have strict rules on how you can promote their products or require a certain amount of traffic or sales to remain in the program. Make sure to read and understand the terms before joining an affiliate program.

Another consideration is the type of commission structure offered by the affiliate program. Some programs offer a one-time commission for each sale, while others offer recurring commissions for subscriptions or membership programs. Depending on your niche and audience, one type of commission structure may be more lucrative than the other.

It's also helpful to research the competition in your niche and see which affiliate programs they are promoting. This can give you an idea of what programs are successful in your niche and which ones you may want to consider promoting as well.

Here's a jump start to your research into the best affiliate program for your and your interests. These are the top 25 affiliate programs as of 2023:

1. Amazon Associates: Amazon's affiliate program that allows you to earn commissions by promoting their products on your website or blog.
2. ShareASale: A large affiliate network that offers a variety of programs in different industries.
3. CJ Affiliate: One of the oldest and most respected affiliate networks, with a wide range of programs in many different niches.
4. eBay Partner Network: The affiliate program for eBay, which allows you to earn commissions by promoting eBay products on your site.
5. Clickbank: An affiliate network that specializes in digital products, such as ebooks, software, and online courses.
6. Rakuten Marketing Affiliates: Another large affiliate network that offers a range of programs in different industries.
7. Commission Junction: One of the largest affiliate networks, with programs in a wide range of niches.
8. Awin: A popular affiliate network with programs in many different niches, including fashion, beauty, travel, and more.
9. FlexOffers: An affiliate network that offers programs in many different niches, including health and wellness, home and garden, and more.
10. Partnerize: A comprehensive affiliate marketing platform that offers programs in many different niches.
11. Avangate Affiliate Network: A global affiliate network that specializes in software and digital products.
12. MaxBounty: A CPA (cost per action) affiliate network that offers programs in many different niches.

13. Skimlinks: An affiliate network that allows you to monetize your content by automatically converting your product links into affiliate links.
14. Impact Radius: An affiliate marketing platform that offers programs in many different niches, including fashion, travel, and more.
15. Bluehost: A popular web hosting provider that offers an affiliate program with high commission rates.
16. HostGator: Another popular web hosting provider that offers an affiliate program with high commission rates.
17. WP Engine: A managed WordPress hosting provider that offers an affiliate program with high commission rates.
18. Shopify Affiliate Program: An affiliate program for the popular e-commerce platform Shopify.
19. Booking.com Affiliate Partner Program: The affiliate program for Booking.com, which allows you to earn commissions by promoting hotel bookings on your site.
20. Expedia Affiliate Program: The affiliate program for Expedia, which allows you to earn commissions by promoting travel bookings on your site.
21. TripAdvisor Affiliate Program: The affiliate program for TripAdvisor, which allows you to earn commissions by promoting hotel and travel bookings on your site.
22. Udemy Affiliate Program: The affiliate program for the online learning platform Udemy.
23. Skillshare Affiliate Program: The affiliate program for the online learning platform Skillshare.
24. Creative Market Affiliate Program: The affiliate program for the online marketplace Creative Market, which sells digital products such as graphics, fonts, and templates.
25. Canva Affiliate Program: The affiliate program for the online graphic design tool Canva.

When promoting affiliate programs, it's important to be transparent with your audience and disclose that you will earn a commission for any sales made through your link. This builds trust with your audience and can lead to more sales in the long run.

Finding the best affiliate programs for your niche and audience requires research, evaluation, and consideration of various factors such as commission rate, product quality, conversion rate, commission structure, and terms and conditions. By promoting high-quality products with a strong commission structure and being transparent with your audience, you can maximize your earnings and build a successful affiliate marketing business.

Chapter 4

Evaluating Affiliate Programs for Quality and Profitability

Once you have identified potential affiliate programs that align with your niche and audience, it's important to evaluate them for quality and profitability. This ensures that you are promoting products or services that your audience will find valuable and that will also generate revenue for you.

The first factor to consider when evaluating affiliate programs is the commission rate. Higher commission rates may be attractive, but it's important to ensure that the products or services being promoted are relevant to your audience and of high quality. A commission rate of 10% on a $1,000 product may be more lucrative than a commission rate of 50% on a $50 product.

Another factor to consider is the conversion rate of the affiliate program. This refers to the percentage of website visitors who make a purchase after clicking through to the product or service being promoted. Programs with high conversion rates typically have high-quality products, effective marketing materials, and a strong reputation.

It's also important to evaluate the reputation of the company offering the affiliate program. Research the company online and read reviews from customers and other affiliates. Look for any red flags or negative reviews that could indicate a problem with the company's products or customer service.

Additionally, consider the promotional materials provided by the affiliate program. High-quality promotional materials, such as banners, graphics, and email templates, can make it easier for you to effectively promote the product or service. Some programs may also offer additional resources, such as training or support, to help you be successful.

Finally, consider the payment terms of the affiliate program. Some programs pay commissions on a regular schedule, while others may require a minimum threshold before payment is issued. Be sure to understand the payment terms before joining an affiliate program to avoid any surprises or delays in receiving commissions.

There are various tools and resources available to help you assess the quality and profitability of an affiliate program, making it easier for you to choose the right ones for your niche. Here are some of the best resources and tools that can help you evaluate affiliate programs and ensure you make the best decisions for your affiliate marketing business:

1. Affiliate Program Directories: There are many affiliate program directories available online, such as AffiliatePrograms.com, OfferVault, and Commission Junction. These directories offer a wealth of information about affiliate programs, including commission rates, cookie duration, payment methods, and more.
2. Product Reviews: Before promoting a product, it's a good idea to research and review the product yourself. This will give you a better understanding of the product's features and benefits, as well as any potential drawbacks. Product reviews can be found on sites such as Amazon, YouTube, and various blogs.
3. Affiliate Program Reviews: Just like with products, there are also affiliate program reviews available online. These reviews can give you insight into the affiliate program's commission rates, payout threshold, payment frequency, and overall reputation. Some popular affiliate program review sites include Affilorama, High Paying Affiliate Programs, and Affiliate Marketing Dude.
4. Google Trends: Google Trends is a powerful tool that can help you determine the popularity of a particular niche or product. By entering keywords related to your niche or product, you can see how often those keywords are searched for on Google. This can give you an idea of how much demand there is for your niche, and whether it's worth promoting.
5. Social Media: Social media platforms such as Facebook, Twitter, and LinkedIn can also be valuable resources for evaluating affiliate programs. By searching for the product or niche you're interested in promoting, you can see what people are saying about it, as well as any potential competitors.

6. Affiliate Networks: Affiliate networks such as ShareASale, Rakuten Marketing, and Awin offer a wide range of affiliate programs to choose from. These networks often provide tools and resources to help affiliates promote products, as well as detailed reporting and analytics to track your earnings.
7. Industry Conferences: Attending industry conferences and events can be a great way to network with other affiliates and learn about the latest trends in affiliate marketing. These events often feature keynote speakers, workshops, and panel discussions that can help you stay current with the latest affiliate marketing strategies.

Overall, evaluating affiliate programs for quality and profitability requires careful consideration of multiple factors. By taking the time to research and evaluate programs, you can ensure that you are promoting high-quality products or services that will generate revenue for your business.

Chapter 4

Choosing the Right Affiliate Programs for Your Niche

Choosing the right affiliate programs is a critical step in your affiliate marketing journey. With so many affiliate programs available, it can be overwhelming to decide which ones to promote on your site. However, selecting the right affiliate programs for your niche can make a significant difference in your earning potential. In this section, we will discuss how to choose the right affiliate programs for your niche.

1. Know Your Audience: The first step in choosing the right affiliate program is to understand your audience's needs and interests. The more you know about your audience, the easier it will be to select the right affiliate programs. Consider what types of products or services your audience is interested in and find affiliate programs that offer those products or services.
2. Research Affiliate Programs: Once you have a clear understanding of your audience, you can begin researching affiliate programs that are relevant to your niche. Look for affiliate programs that offer high commissions, quality products, and excellent customer service. Check to see if the affiliate program offers marketing materials and tools that will help you promote their products effectively.
3. Evaluate Commission Rates: Commission rates are an essential factor to consider when choosing affiliate programs. You want to select programs that offer a high commission rate, but also keep in mind that higher commission rates may also mean a more competitive market. Consider the commission rate along with the conversion rate, as this will give you an idea of how profitable the affiliate program will be.
4. Check Product Quality: The products or services you promote reflect on your brand and reputation. Therefore, it is crucial to choose affiliate programs that offer quality products or services. Research the products or services offered by the affiliate program, read reviews, and test them yourself before promoting them on your site.

5. Evaluate Affiliate Program Policies: Before joining an affiliate program, it is essential to read and understand their policies. Check if the affiliate program has any restrictions on promotion methods, payment methods, or geographical location. Make sure you can comply with all the requirements of the affiliate program to avoid any issues down the road.
6. Look for Long-Term Partnerships: Building a long-term partnership with an affiliate program is beneficial for both parties. Look for programs that offer recurring commissions, as this can lead to long-term passive income. Also, choose programs that offer a variety of products or services to promote, so you can continue to earn commissions as your audience's needs evolve.
7. Consider the Affiliate Network: Affiliate networks can provide you with access to a variety of affiliate programs. However, not all networks are created equal. Research the network's reputation and performance before joining. Look for networks that offer excellent support, easy-to-use platforms, and a variety of high-quality affiliate programs.

Choosing the right affiliate programs for your niche is critical to your success as an affiliate marketer. By considering the factors outlined in this section, you can make informed decisions and select programs that will help you achieve your earning potential.

Chapter 5: Understanding Affiliate Marketing Terminology

Chapter 5

Understanding Affiliate Marketing Terms

Affiliate marketing can be a profitable way to earn passive income online, but it comes with a unique set of terms and jargon that can be confusing for beginners. Understanding these terms is crucial to your success as an affiliate marketer. In this section, we will break down some of the most common affiliate marketing terms and explain their meaning.

First, let's start with the basics. Affiliate marketing is a performance-based marketing strategy where an affiliate promotes a product or service and earns a commission for each sale made through their unique referral link. The commission can be a percentage of the sale or a flat fee, and it varies depending on the affiliate program.

One of the most important terms in affiliate marketing is the affiliate link. This is a unique URL provided by the affiliate program that contains a tracking code. When a customer clicks on an affiliate link and makes a purchase, the tracking code is used to identify which affiliate referred the customer and attribute the commission accordingly.

Conversion rate is another important term to understand. This refers to the percentage of website visitors who take a desired action, such as making a purchase or filling out a lead form. As an affiliate marketer, it's essential to promote products and services that have a high conversion rate to maximize your earnings.

Another key term is the cookie duration. This is the length of time that the tracking cookie remains on a customer's device after they click on an affiliate link. The longer the cookie duration, the higher the likelihood that the customer will make a purchase and earn the affiliate a commission.

Other important terms to know include affiliate manager, payout threshold, promotional materials, and sub-affiliate. By familiarizing yourself with these terms and understanding their meanings, you'll be better equipped to navigate the world of affiliate marketing and make informed decisions about which programs to promote.

It's worth noting that different affiliate programs may use slightly different terms or have their own unique jargon. Make sure to read through the program's terms and conditions and reach out to the affiliate manager if you have any questions.

There are several tools and resources available that can help you better understand and navigate affiliate marketing terms. By using these tools and resources, you can improve your understanding of affiliate marketing terms and concepts, which can help you become a more successful affiliate marketer. Here are a few:

1. Glossary of Affiliate Marketing Terms: Many affiliate marketing websites and blogs have a glossary of terms specific to the industry. This can be a helpful resource to refer to when you come across unfamiliar terms.
2. Affiliate Marketing Forums: Online forums such as the Warrior Forum and Affilorama have active communities of affiliate marketers who share tips, insights, and resources. These forums can be a great place to ask questions and get advice from experienced marketers.
3. Affiliate Marketing Courses: There are several courses available online that provide in-depth training on affiliate marketing, including an explanation of key terms and concepts. Some popular courses include Wealthy Affiliate, Authority Hacker, and Commission Hero.
4. Affiliate Marketing Podcasts: There are several podcasts that cover topics related to affiliate marketing, including terminology. Some popular ones include The Affiliate Guy Daily, Smart Passive Income, and The Side Hustle Show.
5. Affiliate Marketing Books: There are many books available on the topic of affiliate marketing, including those that cover terminology and concepts. Some recommended titles include "Affiliate Marketing for Beginners" by Evgenii Prussakov, "The Complete Guide to Affiliate Marketing on the Web" by Bruce C. Brown, and "Affiliate Marketing: Launch a Six Figure Business with Clickbank Products" by Adam Wolf.

Learning the essential affiliate marketing terms and their meanings is crucial for any novice looking to start in this industry. By having a solid understanding of these terms, you will be better equipped to navigate the world of affiliate marketing and make informed decisions about which affiliate programs to join and which products to promote.

Don't be intimidated by the jargon, take the time to educate yourself and build a strong foundation that will help you succeed in your affiliate marketing endeavors. Remember, the key to success in affiliate marketing is staying informed, adapting to changes in the industry, and providing value to your audience through quality content and thoughtful product recommendations.

Chapter 5

How Affiliate Networks Work

Affiliate networks serve as a middleman between advertisers and publishers in the affiliate marketing industry. They offer a platform where advertisers can promote their products or services and publishers can earn commissions by promoting those products or services to their audience. In this section, we'll explore how affiliate networks work and how you can use them to your advantage as an affiliate marketer.

At its core, an affiliate network is a marketplace that connects advertisers with publishers. Advertisers sign up with the network to promote their products or services and offer commissions to publishers who successfully promote those products or services. Publishers sign up with the network to find products or services to promote and earn commissions for any sales or leads they generate.

One of the main benefits of using an affiliate network is the convenience it offers. Instead of having to reach out to individual advertisers and negotiate commission rates, publishers can browse through a network's marketplace and find products or services that fit their niche. Similarly, advertisers can rely on the network's technology to track conversions, monitor their campaigns, and manage their affiliate relationships.

Affiliate networks typically offer a variety of tools and resources to help publishers succeed, including tracking links, banners, and other creatives to promote products. They may also offer reporting and analytics tools to help publishers track their performance and optimize their campaigns.

It's important to note that affiliate networks take a percentage of commissions earned by publishers as a fee for their services. This fee varies by network, but it's typically around 20% to 30% of the commission earned by the publisher.

Another important aspect of affiliate networks is their role in managing the relationship between advertisers and publishers. They handle payments, ensure compliance with advertising guidelines and regulations, and resolve any disputes that may arise between the two parties.

Some popular affiliate networks include Commission Junction, ShareASale, ClickBank, and Amazon Associates. Each network has its own strengths and weaknesses, so it's important to research and compare different options to find the one that best suits your needs as an affiliate marketer.

Affiliate networks are a key component of the affiliate marketing industry. They offer a convenient platform for advertisers to promote their products and services and for publishers to earn commissions by promoting those products and services to their audience. By understanding how affiliate networks work and how to use them effectively, you can take your affiliate marketing efforts to the next level and increase your passive income potential.

Chapter 5

Understanding Commission Structures

When it comes to affiliate marketing, understanding commission structures is a crucial aspect of determining your potential earnings. Commission structures determine how much you will earn for each sale or action that is generated through your affiliate link.

There are several different commission structures that you may encounter when working with affiliate programs. One common type of commission structure is a percentage-based commission, where you earn a percentage of the sale amount. For example, if you promote a product that sells for $100 and the commission rate is 10%, you will earn $10 for each sale generated through your affiliate link.

Another common commission structure is a flat-rate commission, where you earn a set amount for each sale or action generated through your affiliate link. This type of commission structure is often used for lower-priced products or for actions such as sign-ups or form completions.

Some affiliate programs may also offer tiered commission structures, where you earn a higher commission rate based on the number of sales or actions generated through your affiliate link. For example, you may earn a commission rate of 10% for the first 10 sales and then a commission rate of 15% for any sales generated after that.

It's important to understand the commission structure of each affiliate program you work with, as well as the potential earnings for each product or service you promote. This can help you determine which affiliate programs are the most profitable for your niche and audience.

When evaluating commission structures, it's also important to consider any additional fees or expenses that may be associated with promoting a particular product or service. For example, some affiliate programs may require you to purchase the product yourself before you can promote it, which can cut into your potential earnings.

Another factor to consider when evaluating commission structures is the length of the cookie duration. The cookie duration refers to the length of time that a user's click on your affiliate link is tracked. A longer cookie duration can increase the likelihood that you will earn a commission if the user makes a purchase later.

In addition to understanding commission structures, it's important to negotiate the best possible commission rates with affiliate programs. This may involve demonstrating your value as an affiliate, such as by showing your website traffic or conversion rates.

Overall, understanding commission structures is essential for maximizing your earnings in affiliate marketing. By evaluating commission rates, additional fees, and cookie durations, as well as negotiating with affiliate programs, you can build a profitable and sustainable affiliate marketing business.

Chapter 6: Creating Great Content to Promote Affiliate Products

Chapter 6

How to Create High-Quality Content

Creating high-quality content is a critical aspect of any successful affiliate marketing strategy. After all, your content is what will drive traffic to your website, engage your audience, and ultimately convince them to make a purchase through your affiliate links. In this section, we will discuss the key elements of high-quality content and provide you with actionable tips to help you create content that will stand out in your niche.

1. Research your topic: Before you start creating your content, it's important to conduct thorough research on your topic. This will help you to understand your audience's needs and preferences, as well as identify any gaps in the market that you can fill with your content.
2. Use engaging headlines: Your headline is the first thing your audience will see, and it's essential to make it catchy and attention-grabbing. Use strong, action-oriented language and highlight the main benefit your content offers.
3. Make it easy to read: Use short paragraphs, bullet points, and subheadings to break up your content into easily digestible chunks. Use a clear and concise writing style and avoid using technical jargon or complicated language.
4. Provide value: Your content should provide value to your audience, whether that's through solving a problem, providing information, or offering entertainment. Aim to provide practical solutions and actionable advice that your audience can use in their lives.
5. Use visuals: Incorporating images, videos, and infographics into your content can help to break up the text and make it more engaging for your audience. Use high-quality visuals that are relevant to your topic and add value to your content.
6. Optimize for SEO: Incorporating relevant keywords into your content can help it to rank higher in search engine results pages (SERPs). Use tools like Google Keyword Planner to identify high-volume, low-competition keywords that you can use in your content.
7. Use social media: Sharing your content on social media can help to drive traffic to your website and increase engagement with your

audience. Use relevant hashtags and engaging captions to promote your content and encourage your followers to share it with their networks.
8. Stay on brand: Your content should reflect your brand's voice and values. Be consistent in your messaging and ensure that your content aligns with your brand's mission and goals.
9. Stay up to date: Keep your content fresh and up to date by regularly updating it with new information, statistics, and insights. This will not only help to keep your audience engaged but will also improve your search engine rankings.

In conclusion, creating high-quality content is a key component of any successful affiliate marketing strategy. By conducting thorough research, using engaging headlines, providing value, using visuals, optimizing for SEO, using social media, staying on brand, and staying up to date, you can create content that will stand out in your niche and drive traffic to your website. Remember, the key to success in affiliate marketing is to provide value to your audience and build trust through high-quality content.

Chapter 6

Using Keywords and SEO to Drive Traffic to Your Site

As an affiliate marketer, driving traffic to your site is essential for success. One effective way to attract visitors is by using keywords and search engine optimization (SEO) techniques. In this section, we'll explore the importance of keywords and SEO and how to use them effectively to drive traffic to your site.

First, let's define what we mean by keywords. Keywords are the terms or phrases that people type into search engines when they're looking for information or products. By identifying and using the right keywords on your website, you can increase your chances of appearing at the top of search engine results pages (SERPs) and attracting more visitors to your site.

To start using keywords effectively, you'll need to conduct keyword research. This involves identifying the most relevant and high-traffic keywords for your niche. There are several tools you can use for this, such as Google's Keyword Planner, Ahrefs, or SEMrush. Once you've identified your target keywords, you can start incorporating them into your content in a natural and organic way. This can include using them in your article headlines, meta descriptions, and throughout your content.

However, it's important to note that keyword stuffing – or overusing keywords in your content – can harm your SEO ranking rather than help it. Search engines have become more sophisticated in recent years, and they can recognize when a site is trying to manipulate its ranking through keyword stuffing. This can result in penalties or even a ban from search engine results altogether. Instead, focus on creating high-quality, informative content that uses keywords naturally and strategically.

In addition to keywords, there are several other SEO techniques you can use to improve your site's ranking and drive traffic. This includes optimizing your website's structure, improving page load times, and ensuring your site is mobile-friendly. It's also important to build high-quality backlinks to your site, which can help establish your site as an authority in your niche and boost your SEO ranking.

Another important aspect of SEO is staying up to date with search engine algorithms and updates. Search engines like Google are constantly evolving, and what worked in the past may no longer be effective. By staying informed about the latest SEO trends and best practices, you can continue to improve your site's ranking and drive more traffic to your site.

There are several free resources and tools available that can help you with keyword research and SEO optimization:

1. Google Keyword Planner - A free tool provided by Google Ads that helps you find relevant keywords for your niche, estimate search traffic, and choose appropriate keywords to target.
2. Google Analytics - A free web analytics service that allows you to track website traffic, user behavior, and other metrics that can help you optimize your website for SEO.
3. SEMrush - A free version of this popular SEO tool provides you with up to 10 keyword searches per day, along with information on keyword difficulty, search volume, and more.
4. Moz Keyword Explorer - Moz offers a free version of its keyword research tool, which provides information on search volume, keyword difficulty, and other metrics to help you choose the best keywords for your content.
5. Yoast SEO - A popular WordPress plugin that helps you optimize your website for SEO, including keyword analysis, meta descriptions, and more.
6. Google Search Console - A free tool that helps you monitor your website's performance in Google search results and provides valuable insights into search queries, clicks, and other metrics.
7. Ahrefs Webmaster Tools - A free suite of SEO tools that includes site audit, backlink analysis, and keyword research features.

Using keywords and SEO techniques can be a powerful way to drive traffic to your affiliate site. By conducting thorough keyword research, incorporating keywords naturally and strategically, and staying current with SEO best practices, you can improve your site's ranking and attract more visitors. With the right approach, you can turn that traffic into valuable leads and sales, and ultimately achieve success as an affiliate marketer.

Chapter 6

How to Write Reviews and Promote Products Effectively

Writing reviews and effectively promoting products is a critical component of affiliate marketing. As an affiliate marketer, your goal is to persuade your audience to purchase a product or service through your unique affiliate link. In this section, we will discuss the key elements of writing compelling reviews and promoting products effectively.

The first step in writing a successful review is to thoroughly research the product you plan to promote. Look for the product's features, benefits, and any potential drawbacks. This information will enable you to provide an honest and accurate review of the product.

When writing a review, it's crucial to be transparent with your audience. Disclose that you're an affiliate and that you'll earn a commission if they purchase through your link. This transparency builds trust with your audience and makes them more likely to buy through your affiliate link.

Your review should provide a comprehensive overview of the product, including its features, benefits, and potential drawbacks. Use clear and concise language and avoid technical jargon that may be difficult for your audience to understand.

In addition to the review itself, it's essential to create a sense of urgency and scarcity in your promotions. Use phrases like "limited time offer" or "only available while supplies last" to encourage your audience to take action quickly.

One of the most effective ways to promote products is through storytelling. Share your personal experiences with the product and explain how it has helped you in your life or business. Personal anecdotes can be powerful motivators for people to make a purchase.

Another critical aspect of effective product promotion is to offer bonuses or incentives to your audience. This could be a free eBook, access to an exclusive Facebook group, or a discount on another product or service you offer. These bonuses can help differentiate your offer from others and encourage your audience to purchase through your link.

It's also essential to optimize your product promotions for search engines. Use keywords relevant to the product in your reviews and descriptions and include the product's name in the URL of your review page. This will help your review rank higher in search results and drive more traffic to your site.

Finally, track your promotions' performance and adjust your strategies accordingly. Use tools like Google Analytics to monitor your website's traffic and sales and analyze your promotions' conversion rates. This information will help you optimize your promotions for maximum effectiveness. Additional tools and resources include:

1. Grammarly: A tool that checks your writing for spelling, grammar, and punctuation errors.
2. Hemingway Editor: A writing tool that helps you simplify your writing and make it more accessible.
3. Yoast SEO: A WordPress plugin that helps you optimize your content for search engines.
4. Canva: A graphic design tool that allows you to create eye-catching images and graphics for your website and social media.
5. Google Analytics: A tool that helps you track your website traffic and understand how users interact with your site.
6. Buzzsumo: A tool that helps you find popular content and influencers in your niche.
7. Amazon Associates Central: The affiliate program for Amazon, which provides a wealth of resources and tools for promoting products on the platform.
8. Commission Junction: An affiliate marketing network that connects publishers with advertisers and provides various tools and resources for managing affiliate programs.
9. ShareASale: Another affiliate marketing network that provides tools and resources for managing affiliate programs.

Effective product promotion requires thorough research, transparency, clear and concise language, a sense of urgency and scarcity, personal storytelling, bonuses or incentives, search engine optimization, and performance tracking. By following these principles, you can write compelling reviews and promote products effectively as an affiliate marketer.

Chapter 7: Maximizing Your Affiliate Earnings

Chapter 7

Tips and Strategies for Increasing Your Affiliate Earnings

As an affiliate marketer, your goal is to increase your earnings and make passive income online. While it may take some time to see significant results, there are several tips and strategies you can implement to accelerate your success. In this section, we'll explore some of the most effective ways to increase your affiliate earnings.

1. Focus on high-paying products: One of the most straightforward ways to increase your earnings is to promote products that offer high commissions. Look for products that offer commissions of at least 30% or higher, as these will provide you with a greater return on your investment of time and effort.
2. Promote recurring commission products: Another effective strategy is to promote products that offer recurring commissions. These are products that customers pay for on a subscription basis, such as software, web hosting, or online courses. By promoting these products, you can earn commissions every time a customer renews their subscription.
3. Use multiple traffic sources: To increase your affiliate earnings, it's essential to diversify your traffic sources. Don't rely solely on one platform or channel to drive traffic to your website. Instead, use a combination of SEO, social media, email marketing, and paid advertising to reach a wider audience.
4. Create valuable content: Your content is what will ultimately drive traffic to your website and convert visitors into customers. Focus on creating high-quality, informative content that provides value to your readers. This will not only increase your traffic but also help to establish you as an authority in your niche.
5. Optimize your affiliate links: It's essential to optimize your affiliate links to ensure that they are generating the maximum amount of revenue for you. Use link cloaking, which disguises your affiliate link as a regular link, and use tracking software to monitor your clicks and conversions.

6. Offer incentives: Consider offering incentives to your readers to encourage them to make a purchase through your affiliate link. This could include offering a bonus or discount for purchasing through your link or providing exclusive content or access to a private group.
7. Stay current with industry trends: The affiliate marketing industry is constantly evolving, so it's essential to stay up to date with the latest trends and strategies. Attend industry events, join affiliate marketing forums, and follow thought leaders in the industry to stay informed and gain valuable insights.
8. Test and optimize your campaigns: Finally, it's crucial to continually test and optimize your campaigns to ensure that you are maximizing your earnings. Test different offers, landing pages, and ad copy to see what works best for your audience, and use data to inform your decisions.

Increasing your affiliate earnings requires dedication, hard work, and a willingness to constantly learn and adapt. By implementing the tips and strategies discussed in this section, you'll be well on your way to maximizing your earnings potential in the affiliate marketing industry.

Remember to focus on creating high-quality content, building relationships with your audience, and promoting products that align with your niche and values. With persistence and a willingness to put in the effort, you can turn your affiliate marketing venture into a successful and profitable source of passive income.

Chapter 7

Leveraging Social Media and Other Channels to Promote Affiliate Products

In today's digital age, social media has become a powerful tool for promoting affiliate products. With billions of active users on various social media platforms, it's essential for affiliate marketers to leverage these channels effectively. In this section, we'll explore some tips and strategies for using social media and other channels to promote affiliate products and increase your earnings.

Firstly, it's important to choose the right social media platforms for your niche. Depending on your target audience, certain platforms may be more effective than others. For example, if your niche is fashion or beauty, Instagram and Pinterest are popular platforms for visual content, while LinkedIn may be more appropriate for business or career-related products.

Once you've identified the appropriate social media platforms, it's important to create engaging content that resonates with your audience. High-quality images, videos, and written content can all be effective in capturing your audience's attention and encouraging them to click on your affiliate links.

In addition to social media, there are other channels you can use to promote affiliate products. Email marketing, for example, can be an effective way to reach your audience directly and promote products through newsletters or dedicated email campaigns. You can also use paid advertising on platforms such as Google Ads or Facebook Ads to target specific audiences and drive traffic to your affiliate links.

Another strategy for leveraging social media and other channels is to collaborate with other influencers or bloggers in your niche. By partnering with others who have a similar audience, you can expand your reach and promote products to a wider audience.

Finally, it's important to track your results and analyze your performance. Tools like Google Analytics can help you monitor your website traffic and track conversions from your affiliate links. This information can help you optimize your campaigns and improve your overall earnings.

There are several tools and resources that can help you effectively leverage social media and other channels to promote affiliate products. By utilizing these tools and resources, you can effectively leverage social media and other channels to promote affiliate products and maximize your earnings. Here are some of them:

1. Hootsuite - This is a social media management platform that allows you to schedule and publish posts across multiple social media platforms, monitor your brand mentions and track your performance metrics.
2. Canva - This is a graphic design tool that can help you create eye-catching and engaging visuals for your social media posts, blog articles and other promotional materials.
3. Buffer - This is a social media management tool that can help you schedule and publish posts across multiple social media platforms, as well as track your performance metrics.
4. Google Analytics - This is a powerful tool that can help you track and analyze your website traffic and user behavior, as well as measure the effectiveness of your marketing campaigns.
5. Bitly - This is a URL shortening and tracking tool that allows you to create custom links for your affiliate products and track clicks and conversions.
6. Email marketing platforms - Email marketing is a powerful way to promote affiliate products and build a loyal audience. Some popular email marketing platforms include Mailchimp, Constant Contact, and ConvertKit.
7. Affiliate networks - Many affiliate networks have their own tools and resources for promoting products, including banners, widgets, and other creatives.
8. BuzzSumo: Research popular and trending topics in your niche and see what content performs best on social media with this content marketing tool.

9. Facebook Ads Manager: Create and run targeted Facebook ads to reach your ideal audience and drive traffic to your affiliate site.
10. YouTube: Use this video-sharing platform to create product reviews and tutorials that can be shared across various social media channels.
11. Reddit: Join relevant subreddits in your niche and participate in discussions to establish yourself as an authority and promote your affiliate products. Recommended subreddits include:
    a. r/Affiliatemarketing - This subreddit is dedicated to all things affiliate marketing, including tips, strategies, and case studies.
    b. r/juststart - This subreddit is focused on helping beginners start and grow their affiliate marketing businesses.
    c. r/SEO - While not specifically focused on affiliate marketing, this subreddit can provide valuable insights into search engine optimization (SEO), which is a critical component of successful affiliate marketing.
    d. r/Entrepreneur - This subreddit is dedicated to entrepreneurship in general, but often features discussions and advice on affiliate marketing.
    e. r/Affiliate - This subreddit is focused on affiliate marketing, including discussions on various affiliate programs, strategies, and tools.
    f. r/WorkOnline - This subreddit is dedicated to finding ways to make money online, including affiliate marketing.
12. Quora: Answer questions related to your niche and link back to your affiliate site or relevant product pages to drive traffic and generate leads.
13. Pinterest: Use this visual search engine to create and share boards featuring your affiliate products and related content.

Leveraging social media and other channels can be a powerful way to promote affiliate products and increase your earnings. By choosing the right platforms, creating engaging content, collaborating with other influencers, and tracking your results, you can effectively promote products and build a successful affiliate marketing business.

Chapter 7

Building Relationships with Your Audience and Affiliate Partners

One of the most important aspects of affiliate marketing is building strong relationships with your audience and affiliate partners. By doing so, you can establish trust, credibility, and loyalty, which can ultimately lead to increased sales and earnings. In this section, we'll explore some effective strategies for building and maintaining relationships with both your audience and affiliate partners.

First and foremost, it's important to understand your audience and their needs. By knowing what they're looking for and what problems they're trying to solve, you can create content that's tailored to their interests and provides value. Engage with your audience through comments, social media, and email to gather feedback and insights that can help you better serve them.

When it comes to your affiliate partners, it's important to communicate effectively and regularly. Keep them updated on your promotions, traffic, and sales performance, and be transparent about any issues or concerns that arise. By maintaining open and honest communication, you can establish a strong working relationship that benefits both parties.

In addition to communication, it's also important to be proactive in promoting your affiliate partners. Share their products or services on your social media channels and in your email newsletters and highlight their offerings in your content. By actively promoting your affiliate partners, you can demonstrate your support and build goodwill.

Another effective strategy for building relationships with your audience and affiliate partners is to offer exclusive promotions or discounts. This can be a win-win for both parties, as it incentivizes your audience to make a purchase and can drive more sales for your affiliate partners. Consider negotiating with your partners to offer special deals or coupons that are only available to your audience.

To build trust and credibility with your audience and affiliate partners, it's also important to be honest and authentic in your recommendations. Only promote products or services that you truly believe in and have personally tried or tested. Avoid promoting products solely for the sake of earning a commission, as this can damage your credibility and erode trust with your audience.

Finally, don't underestimate the power of gratitude and appreciation. Take the time to thank your audience and affiliate partners for their support and loyalty, whether it's through a personalized email, a shoutout on social media, or a small gift or token of appreciation. By showing your gratitude, you can foster positive relationships and build a strong community around your brand.

Here are some tools and resources that can help you build relationships with your audience and affiliate partners:

1. Email marketing software: Email marketing is an effective way to build and maintain relationships with your audience. Tools like Mailchimp, ConvertKit, and AWeber can help you create and send newsletters, promotional emails, and other types of email campaigns.
2. Social media management tools: Social media can be a powerful tool for building relationships with your audience and promoting your affiliate products. Tools like Hootsuite, Buffer, and Sprout Social can help you manage and schedule your social media posts, engage with your followers, and track your social media performance.
3. Affiliate networks: Joining an affiliate network can help you build relationships with affiliate partners and promote a wide range of products and services. Some of the top affiliate networks include ShareASale, Commission Junction, and Rakuten Marketing.
4. Online communities: Participating in online communities like forums and Facebook groups can help you connect with other affiliate marketers and potential customers. Look for communities that are relevant to your niche and engage in conversations and share your expertise.

5. Content creation tools: Creating high-quality content is key to building relationships with your audience and driving traffic to your affiliate links. Tools like Canva, Grammarly, and Hemingway can help you create engaging content that resonates with your audience.
6. Relationship management software: Managing relationships with your affiliate partners can be challenging, especially if you work with multiple partners. Tools like Ambassador and Partnerize can help you manage your affiliate relationships, track commissions, and monitor performance.

Building relationships with your audience and affiliate partners is a crucial component of success in affiliate marketing. By understanding your audience's needs, communicating effectively with your partners, promoting their products or services, and being honest and authentic in your recommendations, you can establish trust, credibility, and loyalty that can lead to increased sales and earnings. And don't forget to show your appreciation and gratitude to those who support you along the way.

Chapter 8: Creating a Sales Funnel for Affiliate Marketing

Chapter 8

Understanding Sales Funnels and How They Work

As a marketer, it's important to understand the concept of sales funnels and how they work. A sales funnel is the journey that a potential customer goes through before making a purchase. It's a series of steps that lead them from being aware of a product to making the final decision to buy it. A well-designed sales funnel can help increase your conversion rates and ultimately, your affiliate earnings.

The first step in building a sales funnel is to create a landing page that captures the visitor's attention and encourages them to take action. This page should be designed to address the visitor's pain points and clearly communicate the benefits of the product or service you are promoting. A strong call-to-action (CTA) is essential to encourage the visitor to take the next step in the funnel.

Once the visitor has taken the desired action on the landing page, such as filling out a form or subscribing to a newsletter, they will be taken to a thank you page. This page should confirm that their action was successful and provide them with additional information or resources that are relevant to the product or service they are interested in.

The next step in the funnel is to nurture the lead by providing them with valuable content that helps to build trust and establish your authority in the niche. This can be in the form of blog posts, email newsletters, webinars, or social media posts. The goal is to keep the lead engaged and interested in the product or service you are promoting.

Once the lead is sufficiently interested, it's time to present them with an offer. This can be a free trial, a discounted price, or a special promotion that is only available for a limited time. The goal is to create a sense of urgency and encourage the lead to act before the offer expires.

If the lead decides to make a purchase, they will be taken to a checkout page where they can complete the transaction. This page should be designed to be as simple and user-friendly as possible to ensure a smooth and hassle-free checkout process.

After the purchase is complete, it's important to follow up with the customer to ensure their satisfaction and encourage them to become a repeat customer. This can be done through email newsletters, customer support, and special promotions that are only available to existing customers.

Here are some comprehensive tools and resources for understanding and implementing sales funnels:

1. ClickFunnels - ClickFunnels is a popular tool for building and managing sales funnels. It offers a wide range of features, including customizable templates, drag-and-drop page builders, email marketing automation, and A/B testing. ClickFunnels also has a large community and support network, making it easy to find resources and guidance on building effective sales funnels.
2. Leadpages - Leadpages is another popular sales funnel tool that allows users to easily create landing pages, pop-ups, and opt-in forms. It includes a drag-and-drop page builder, A/B testing, and email marketing integration. Leadpages also offers a variety of templates and resources to help users build effective sales funnels.
3. Infusionsoft - Infusionsoft is a comprehensive CRM and marketing automation tool that includes a built-in sales funnel builder. It offers features like lead scoring, automated email campaigns, and sales pipeline management, as well as integrations with other tools like social media and e-commerce platforms.
4. ConvertKit - ConvertKit is an email marketing tool that also includes a basic sales funnel builder. It offers features like customizable landing pages, opt-in forms, and email automation. ConvertKit is popular among bloggers and online creators who want to build a relationship with their audience through email marketing.
5. Funnel Scripts - Funnel Scripts is a tool that helps users write effective copy for their sales funnels. It includes templates and scripts for various stages of the funnel, including opt-in pages, sales

pages, and upsell pages. Funnel Scripts is a helpful resource for those who struggle with writing persuasive and effective copy.

6. Udemy - Udemy offers a wide range of courses on sales funnels and related topics, such as email marketing and copywriting. These courses can provide a comprehensive education on building and optimizing effective sales funnels.
7. ClickBank University - ClickBank University is an online education platform that offers courses on affiliate marketing and sales funnel building. It includes training on topics like product creation, funnel building, and driving traffic to your sales funnel.
8. Neil Patel - Neil Patel is a well-known digital marketing expert who provides a wealth of free resources on his website, including articles and videos on sales funnels and related topics. His website is a great resource for those looking to learn more about sales funnel optimization and digital marketing in general.
9. Funnel Hacking Live: Funnel Hacking Live is an annual event hosted by ClickFunnels. It offers training and networking opportunities for those interested in sales funnel optimization.
10. The Funnel Hacker's Cookbook: The Funnel Hacker's Cookbook is a book by Russell Brunson, the founder of ClickFunnels. It provides a comprehensive guide to sales funnel design and optimization.
11. Funnel University: Funnel University is a training program by ClickFunnels that offers in-depth training on sales funnel design and optimization.
12. The Sales Funnel Podcast: The Sales Funnel Podcast is a podcast hosted by David Abrams that covers topics related to sales funnel design, optimization, and marketing.

Understanding sales funnels is essential to the success of your affiliate marketing efforts. By creating a well-designed sales funnel, you can increase your conversion rates and ultimately, your affiliate earnings. Remember to focus on capturing the visitor's attention, nurturing the lead, presenting them with an offer, and following up with the customer to ensure their satisfaction. With these strategies in place, you can create a highly effective sales funnel that drives results for your affiliate marketing business.

Chapter 8

Creating Your Own Sales Funnel for Affiliate Marketing

If you want to make the most out of your affiliate marketing efforts, creating your own sales funnel can help you achieve your goals. A sales funnel is a step-by-step process that guides your potential customers towards a purchase decision. By creating a sales funnel for your affiliate marketing efforts, you can improve your conversions and earn more commissions.

Here are some steps to help you create your own sales funnel for affiliate marketing:

1. Identify Your Target Audience: The first step in creating a sales funnel for affiliate marketing is to identify your target audience. Who are the people you want to reach with your marketing efforts? What are their needs, interests, and pain points? By understanding your target audience, you can create content that resonates with them and guides them towards a purchase decision.
2. Choose Your Affiliate Products: Next, choose the affiliate products you want to promote. Look for products that are relevant to your target audience and that offer high commissions. You should also consider the quality of the products and the reputation of the affiliate program you're working with.
3. Create Your Landing Page: A landing page is a standalone page that is designed to convert visitors into leads or customers. Create a landing page that showcases the benefits of the affiliate product you're promoting and encourages visitors to take action. Use compelling copy and visuals to grab their attention and persuade them to click through to the product page.
4. Drive Traffic to Your Landing Page: Once you've created your landing page, you need to drive traffic to it. There are many ways to drive traffic to your landing page, including social media, paid advertising, email marketing, and content marketing. Choose the strategies that work best for your target audience and budget.
5. Follow Up with Email Marketing: Email marketing is a powerful tool for nurturing leads and guiding them towards a purchase

decision. Use an email marketing tool to create a series of automated emails that provide value to your subscribers and promote the affiliate products you're promoting. Make sure your emails are relevant and engaging, and always include a clear call to action.

6. Add Upsells and Downsells: Upsells and downsells are additional products or services that you offer to your customers after they make a purchase. Upsells are products that are more expensive than the original purchase, while downsells are products that are less expensive. By adding upsells and downsells to your sales funnel, you can increase your revenue per customer.
7. Measure Your Results: Finally, it's important to measure your results so you can optimize your sales funnel for better conversions. Use analytics tools to track your traffic, conversions, and revenue. Look for areas where you can improve your sales funnel, such as optimizing your landing page or improving your email marketing campaigns.

There are a variety of resources available to help you learn how to create your own sales funnel for affiliate marketing. Here are some recommended ones:

1. ClickFunnels: ClickFunnels is a popular platform that provides comprehensive tools for building sales funnels. They offer a range of resources including training courses, webinars, and a community forum to help you learn and optimize your funnel building skills.
2. Udemy: Udemy is an online learning platform that offers courses on a wide range of topics, including sales funnel creation. Some recommended courses for affiliate marketers include "Sales Funnel Mastery: The Bridge Page Sales Funnel" and "ClickFunnels: Sales Funnels & Landing Pages Made Easy".
3. YouTube: There are many YouTube channels that offer free tutorials and advice on creating sales funnels. Some popular channels include "ClickFunnels" and "Russell Brunson".
4. Funnel Hacks: Funnel Hacks is a comprehensive training program that teaches you how to create high-converting sales funnels. They offer a range of resources including courses, templates, and coaching to help you optimize your funnel-building skills.

5. Affiliate Marketing Mastery: Affiliate Marketing Mastery is a training program that focuses specifically on affiliate marketing. They offer a range of resources including courses, webinars, and a community forum to help you learn and grow your affiliate marketing business, including creating your own sales funnel.

Creating your own sales funnel for affiliate marketing can help you earn more commissions and improve your conversions. By following the steps outlined above, you can create a sales funnel that is tailored to your target audience and that guides them towards a purchase decision. Remember to always track your results and optimize your sales funnel for better performance.

Chapter 8

Maximizing Your Profits with a Sales Funnel

In affiliate marketing, a sales funnel is an essential tool to maximize your profits. A sales funnel is a series of steps designed to guide a potential customer towards making a purchase. The goal of a sales funnel is to convert as many visitors as possible into paying customers. In this section, we will discuss how to maximize your profits with a sales funnel.

1. Optimize Your Landing Page: Your landing page is the first page a potential customer sees when they click on your affiliate link. It is essential to optimize your landing page to make a good first impression. Make sure your landing page is visually appealing, has clear and concise copy, and is easy to navigate.
2. Create an Irresistible Offer: An irresistible offer is an offer that is so good that a potential customer cannot resist it. An irresistible offer could be a discount, a free trial, or a free eBook. An irresistible offer can help you convert more visitors into paying customers.
3. Use an Autoresponder: An autoresponder is an email marketing tool that allows you to send automated emails to potential customers. Use an autoresponder to follow up with potential customers who have expressed interest in your product or service. This can help you convert more visitors into paying customers.
4. Upsell and Cross-sell: Once a customer has made a purchase, use upselling and cross-selling to increase your profits. Upselling is the process of offering a more expensive product or service, while cross-selling is the process of offering a related product or service.
5. Use Retargeting Ads: Retargeting ads are ads that are shown to people who have previously visited your website. Retargeting ads can help you bring back potential customers who did not make a purchase the first time they visited your website.
6. Test and Optimize: It is essential to test and optimize your sales funnel regularly. Use analytics tools to track your sales funnel's performance and make changes as needed.
7. Provide Excellent Customer Service: Excellent customer service is crucial to maximizing your profits with a sales funnel. Make sure

you respond promptly to customer inquiries and address any concerns or complaints.
8. Continuously Improve Your Offer: Continuously improving your offer can help you maximize your profits with a sales funnel. Use customer feedback to make changes to your offer and ensure it remains irresistible to potential customers.
9. Monitor Your Competition: Monitoring your competition can help you stay ahead of the game. Keep an eye on what your competitors are doing and adjust your sales funnel accordingly.

There are many great YouTube videos and channels that can help you learn more about maximizing your profits with a sales funnel. These channels provide valuable insights into the world of sales funnels and can help you take your affiliate marketing efforts to the next level. Here are some recommendations:

1. ClickFunnels: This channel is dedicated to teaching people how to use the ClickFunnels platform to create and optimize their sales funnels. They have a wide range of tutorials and training videos that cover everything from building landing pages to creating automated email sequences.
2. Russell Brunson: As the founder of ClickFunnels, Russell Brunson is a leading expert on sales funnels. His YouTube channel features a mix of tutorials, case studies, and interviews with other successful entrepreneurs.
3. Neil Patel: Neil Patel is a well-known digital marketing expert who has created several videos on how to use sales funnels to increase your profits. His channel covers a wide range of topics related to digital marketing, including SEO, social media, and email marketing.
4. Miles Beckler: Miles Beckler is a digital marketing strategist who has helped thousands of entrepreneurs grow their businesses using sales funnels. His YouTube channel features a mix of tutorials, case studies, and interviews with other successful marketers.
5. Pat Flynn: Pat Flynn is a successful affiliate marketer and entrepreneur who has built a loyal following through his Smart Passive Income brand. His YouTube channel features a mix of

tutorials, interviews, and case studies that cover a wide range of topics related to online business, including sales funnels.

A sales funnel is an essential tool for maximizing your profits in affiliate marketing. By optimizing your landing page, creating an irresistible offer, using an autoresponder, upselling and cross-selling, retargeting ads, testing & optimizing, providing excellent customer service, continuously improving your offer, and monitoring your competition, you can create a sales funnel that converts visitors into paying customers and maximizes your profits.

Chapter 9: Using Paid Advertising to Promote Affiliate Products

Chapter 9

Understanding Paid Advertising

Paid advertising is a powerful tool that can help you reach your target audience and drive traffic to your website. However, it can also be intimidating and overwhelming for those new to affiliate marketing. In this section, we'll break down the basics of paid advertising and give you some tips on how to use it effectively.

First, let's define what paid advertising is. Paid advertising is any form of advertising that you pay for, such as pay-per-click (PPC) advertising, display advertising, or social media advertising. These ads typically appear on search engines, websites, or social media platforms and are designed to drive traffic to your website.

One of the most popular forms of paid advertising is PPC advertising, which allows you to bid on specific keywords and phrases related to your niche. When someone searches for those keywords, your ad will appear at the top of the search results. You only pay when someone clicks on your ad, making it a cost-effective way to drive traffic to your site.

Another form of paid advertising is display advertising, which involves placing ads on other websites that are relevant to your niche. These ads can be in the form of banners, pop-ups, or video ads, and they can be targeted to specific audiences based on their browsing history and demographics.

Social media advertising is also becoming increasingly popular, as it allows you to target specific audiences based on their interests, behaviors, and demographics. You can run ads on platforms like Facebook, Instagram, and Twitter, and you only pay when someone clicks on your ad or takes a specific action, like filling out a form or making a purchase.

When it comes to using paid advertising for affiliate marketing, it's important to have a clear strategy in place. You'll want to identify your target audience, research relevant keywords and phrases, and create compelling ad copy and visuals that will grab their attention and entice them to click through to your site.

It's also important to track your results and adjust as needed. This means monitoring your ad spend, analyzing your conversion rates, and optimizing your ads to improve their performance over time.

In terms of budgeting for paid advertising, it's best to start small and gradually increase your spending as you see results. Set a daily or weekly budget and stick to it and be sure to measure your ROI to ensure that your advertising dollars are being well-spent.

Here are some YouTube channels, blogs, and podcasts that cover the topic of paid advertising:

1. PPC University - This YouTube channel offers a comprehensive guide to pay-per-click (PPC) advertising. The channel is run by WordStream, a digital marketing agency that specializes in PPC advertising.
2. AdEspresso - AdEspresso is a blog that covers a variety of topics related to social media advertising, including Facebook, Instagram, and Google ads. They also offer a lot of helpful guides and tutorials on their website.
3. Google Ads - The official Google Ads YouTube channel offers a lot of helpful videos for beginners who are just getting started with paid advertising on Google. They cover topics like creating ad campaigns, setting up targeting options, and analyzing your results.
4. WordStream - The WordStream blog covers a wide range of topics related to online advertising, including PPC advertising, social media advertising, and display advertising. They also offer a lot of helpful resources like eBooks and webinars.
5. Facebook Business - The official Facebook Business YouTube channel offers a lot of helpful videos for advertisers who want to learn more about Facebook ads. They cover topics like ad formats, targeting options, and analytics.
6. AdRoll - AdRoll is a digital marketing platform that specializes in retargeting and display advertising. Their blog covers a variety of

topics related to online advertising, including best practices for ad creatives, targeting options, and audience segmentation.
7. HubSpot - HubSpot is a popular marketing platform that offers a variety of tools for inbound marketing and sales. Their blog covers a wide range of topics related to online marketing, including paid advertising.
8. Perpetual Traffic by DigitalMarketer - This podcast covers a variety of digital marketing topics, including paid advertising. They provide tips and strategies for running effective ad campaigns and maximizing your ROI.
9. The Art of Paid Traffic by Rick Mulready - This podcast is focused specifically on paid advertising, covering topics such as Facebook ads, Google AdWords, and more. They interview experts in the field and provide practical tips for improving your campaigns.
10. Online Marketing Made Easy with Amy Porterfield - While not exclusively focused on paid advertising, this podcast covers a wide range of digital marketing topics, including paid advertising. Amy Porterfield provides practical tips and strategies for running successful campaigns.
11. The Paid Search Podcast by Chris Schaeffer and Jason Rothman - This podcast is focused specifically on Google AdWords and provides tips and strategies for optimizing your campaigns and increasing conversions.
12. The Paid Search Magic Podcast by Daniel K Cheung - This podcast covers a range of topics related to paid advertising, including Google AdWords, Facebook ads, and more. They interview experts in the field and provide practical advice for running successful campaigns.

Ultimately, paid advertising can be a powerful tool for driving traffic and generating sales for your affiliate marketing business. By understanding the basics and developing a clear strategy, you can maximize your results and see a significant return on your investment.

Chapter 9

Choosing the Right Advertising Channels

Choosing the right advertising channels is crucial to the success of any affiliate marketing campaign. With so many options available, it can be overwhelming to determine which channels will be the most effective for your specific audience and goals. In this section, we will explore some of the most popular advertising channels and provide tips for selecting the right ones for your affiliate marketing strategy.

One of the most popular advertising channels is Google Ads. With Google Ads, you can display ads on Google search results pages, as well as on other websites that are part of the Google Display Network. Google Ads uses a pay-per-click model, so you only pay when someone clicks on your ad. This can be an effective way to drive targeted traffic to your website, but it can also be expensive if you don't target your keywords carefully.

Another popular advertising channel is Facebook Ads. With Facebook Ads, you can create ads that appear in the Facebook news feed or on Instagram. Facebook Ads uses a variety of targeting options, including age, gender, location, interests, and behaviors. This can be an effective way to reach a specific audience, but it's important to monitor your ad spend to ensure that you're not overspending on clicks that don't convert.

Instagram Ads is another popular advertising channel, particularly for affiliate marketing campaigns that target younger audiences. Instagram Ads allow you to display ads in users' feeds or in Stories, with the ability to target users based on their interests and behaviors. Instagram Ads also use a pay-per-click model, so you only pay when someone clicks on your ad.

YouTube Ads is another popular advertising channel that allows you to display video ads to YouTube users. YouTube Ads use a pay-per-view model, so you only pay when someone views your ad. This can be an effective way to reach a large audience, but it's important to create compelling video content that will keep viewers engaged.

In addition to these popular advertising channels, there are many other options available, such as Twitter Ads, LinkedIn Ads, and Pinterest Ads. When choosing the right advertising channels for your affiliate marketing campaign, it's important to consider your audience, your budget, and your goals. You should also test different channels to determine which ones are the most effective for driving conversions and maximizing your ROI.

To maximize the effectiveness of your advertising campaigns, it's also important to track your results and adjust as needed. Use tools like Google Analytics or Facebook Ads Manager to monitor your ad spend and track your conversions. Use A/B testing to determine which ad copy, images, or targeting options are the most effective for driving clicks and conversions. Here are some YouTube videos that compare different ad networks:

1. "Google Ads vs Facebook Ads: Which Paid Advertising Should You Use for Online Marketing?" by Neil Patel: In this video, Neil Patel compares Google Ads and Facebook Ads and provides insights on which one to choose based on your business objectives and target audience.
2. "Google Ads vs. Bing Ads (2021) | Which PPC Advertising Platform is Better?" by Surfside PPC: This video compares Google Ads and Bing Ads and highlights the key differences between the two platforms, including audience reach, targeting options, and cost.
3. "Instagram Ads vs Facebook Ads - Which is Better for Affiliate Marketing?" by John Crestani: John Crestani compares Instagram Ads and Facebook Ads and provides tips on how to leverage each platform for affiliate marketing.
4. "YouTube Ads vs Facebook Ads - Which One Should You Use?" by Justin Bryant: In this video, Justin Bryant compares YouTube Ads and Facebook Ads and helps viewers decide which platform to choose based on their advertising goals and budget.
5. "Native Ads vs. Facebook Ads - Which is Better?" by Voluum DSP: This video compares native ads and Facebook ads and provides insights on which platform to choose based on your target audience and advertising budget.

6. "Amazon Ads vs. Google Ads: Which One Should You Use?" by Jungle Scout: This video compares Amazon Ads and Google Ads and provides insights on which platform to choose based on your product and target audience.

Keep in mind that the effectiveness of an ad network can vary depending on your niche, target audience, and advertising budget. It's important to experiment with different platforms to see which one works best for your business.

Ultimately, the key to success with advertising channels in affiliate marketing is to stay focused on your audience and your goals. Keep experimenting with different channels and tactics until you find the ones that work best for your specific campaign. And always remember to monitor your results and adjust as needed to optimize your campaigns and maximize your profits.

Chapter 9

Creating Effective Ads for Affiliate Marketing

Creating effective ads for affiliate marketing is an essential component of a successful advertising campaign. While there is no one-size-fits-all approach, there are several tips and strategies that can help you create ads that are both attention-grabbing and effective.

First, it's important to understand your audience and what motivates them. This can help you tailor your ad messaging and visuals to their specific needs and desires. For example, if your target audience is interested in fitness, your ad could feature an athlete using the product or a before-and-after transformation photo.

Next, make sure your ad has a clear and compelling call-to-action (CTA). This can be a button or a sentence that encourages users to take a specific action, such as "Shop Now" or "Sign Up for Our Newsletter". A clear CTA can increase click-through rates and ultimately lead to more conversions.

Another key aspect of creating effective ads is the use of visuals. High-quality images and videos can grab the attention of your audience and make your ad more engaging. Make sure your visuals are relevant to your product and audience and are of high quality.

In addition to visuals, the ad copy is also crucial. Your ad copy should be concise, clear, and compelling. It should highlight the benefits of the product and what sets it apart from competitors. Use action-oriented language and avoid industry jargon or technical terms that your audience may not understand.

Testing and analyzing your ads is also important to ensure their effectiveness. You can experiment with different ad formats, messaging, and visuals to see what resonates best with your audience. Use analytics tools to track the performance of your ads and make adjustments as needed.

It's also important to keep your brand voice consistent across all of your ads and marketing materials. This can help build trust and recognition with your audience. Consistency in messaging and visuals can also help create a cohesive and memorable brand identity.

Finally, be sure to comply with advertising regulations and guidelines. This includes disclosing your affiliate relationships and following any rules related to advertising specific products or services.

There are various tools and resources that can help you create effective ads for your affiliate marketing campaigns. By using these tools and resources, you can create effective ads that attract potential customers and drive conversions for your affiliate marketing campaigns. Here are some recommendations:

1. Canva: Canva is a free graphic design tool that allows you to create professional-looking images for your ads. You can choose from a variety of templates and customize them to fit your brand.
2. Unsplash: Unsplash is a platform that offers high-quality stock photos that you can use for your ads. The images are free and can be downloaded and used without attribution.
3. Google Ads Editor: Google Ads Editor is a free tool provided by Google that allows you to create and edit your ads in bulk. You can make changes to your campaigns offline and then upload them when you're ready to launch.
4. Facebook Ads Manager: Facebook Ads Manager is a tool that allows you to create and manage your Facebook ads. You can target specific audiences, set a budget, and track your results.
5. A/B testing tools: A/B testing is a process of testing different versions of your ads to see which one performs better. There are various tools available, such as Google Optimize and Optimizely, that allow you to set up and run A/B tests.
6. Persado: This AI platform uses natural language processing and machine learning to generate data-driven ad copy that resonates with your target audience.
7. Albert: This AI tool leverages predictive analytics and machine learning to optimize your ad campaigns across multiple channels, including social media, search, and display.

8. Phrasee: This AI-powered copywriting tool uses natural language generation to create high-performing ad copy that is tailored to your brand's unique voice and messaging.
9. Adext: This AI-based platform uses deep learning algorithms to optimize your ad campaigns in real-time, with the goal of maximizing conversions and reducing ad spend.
10. Receptiviti: This AI tool uses psycholinguistics and natural language processing to analyze your target audience's personality traits and emotional responses, allowing you to create ads that resonate on a deeper level.

Creating effective ads for affiliate marketing involves understanding your audience, using clear and compelling messaging, incorporating high-quality visuals, testing & analyzing performance, maintaining consistency in branding, and adhering to advertising regulations. By following these strategies, you can create ads that are both effective and profitable for your affiliate marketing business.

Chapter 10: Scaling Your Affiliate Marketing Business

Chapter 10

How to Grow Your Affiliate Marketing Business

Congratulations on making it this far in your affiliate marketing journey! By now, you should have a good understanding of the basics of affiliate marketing and the different strategies you can use to promote products and earn commissions. However, the journey doesn't end here. In this section, we'll explore some tips and strategies for growing your affiliate marketing business and taking it to the next level.

1. Build your email list: Your email list is one of the most valuable assets of your affiliate marketing business. By capturing the email addresses of your visitors, you can build a list of targeted prospects who are interested in the products you promote. Use lead magnets, such as free eBooks or webinars, to incentivize visitors to sign up for your list. Once you have a list, use email marketing to nurture relationships and promote products.
2. Create content consistently: Consistency is key when it comes to building a successful affiliate marketing business. Create content regularly, whether it's blog posts, videos, or social media posts. Your content should be high-quality and provide value to your audience. This will help you establish yourself as an authority in your niche and attract a loyal following.
3. Diversify your income streams: While affiliate marketing can be a lucrative business, it's important to diversify your income streams. Consider creating your own digital products, such as eBooks or courses, or offering consulting services in your niche. This will not only provide additional income, but also help you establish yourself as an expert in your field.
4. Use paid advertising strategically: Paid advertising can be a powerful tool for driving traffic and increasing conversions, but it can also be costly if not used strategically. Consider starting small and testing different ad campaigns to see what works best for your audience. Use retargeting ads to reach visitors who have shown interest in your products but haven't made a purchase yet.

5. Attend industry events and network with others: Networking is important in any industry, and affiliate marketing is no exception. Attend industry events, such as conferences or trade shows, to connect with other affiliate marketers and learn about the latest trends and strategies. Join online communities or forums where you can exchange ideas and learn from others.
6. Continuously track and analyze your results: To grow your affiliate marketing business, it's important to continuously track and analyze your results. Use analytics tools to measure your website traffic, conversion rates, and earnings. This will help you identify areas for improvement and make data-driven decisions.
7. Stay current with industry trends and changes: The affiliate marketing industry is constantly evolving, with new trends and changes emerging all the time. Stay up to date with the latest news and developments by following industry publications, attending webinars or online courses, and participating in online communities.
8. Build relationships with your audience and partners: As we discussed earlier, building relationships is crucial for success in affiliate marketing. Continue to nurture relationships with your audience by providing value and engaging with them regularly. Also, build strong relationships with your affiliate partners by communicating regularly and negotiating mutually beneficial terms.
9. Set realistic goals and be patient: Finally, remember that building a successful affiliate marketing business takes time and effort. Set realistic goals for your business and be patient as you work towards achieving them. Celebrate your successes along the way and learn from your failures.

Here are some recommended free tools and resources for outsourcing and automating tasks in affiliate marketing. These tools can help you streamline your affiliate marketing tasks, save time and effort, and focus on growing your business:

1. Trello: This is a free project management tool that can help you organize your tasks and projects. You can use it to collaborate with your team, create to-do lists, and keep track of deadlines.

2. Hootsuite: This is a free social media management tool that can help you automate your social media tasks. You can use it to schedule posts, monitor your social media accounts, and track your social media performance.
3. Canva: This is a free graphic design tool that can help you create stunning visuals for your affiliate marketing campaigns. You can use it to create images for your social media posts, blog posts, and email newsletters.
4. Google Analytics: This is a free web analytics tool that can help you track your website traffic and user behavior. You can use it to analyze your website performance, identify your top-performing pages, and optimize your website for better conversions.
5. Zapier: This is a free automation tool that can help you connect different apps and automate your workflows. You can use it to automate repetitive tasks, integrate your apps, and save time and effort.
6. HubSpot CRM: This is a free customer relationship management tool that can help you manage your contacts and leads. You can use it to track your sales pipeline, manage your customer interactions, and analyze your sales performance.
7. Toggl: This is a free time tracking tool that can help you measure your productivity and efficiency. You can use it to track your time on different tasks, analyze your work habits, and improve your time management skills.

As you can see, there are many ways to grow your affiliate marketing business and increase your passive income. The key is to be consistent, patient, and always willing to learn and adapt to the changing landscape of affiliate marketing. With the right strategies and tools, you can turn your affiliate marketing business into a profitable and sustainable source of income.

Chapter 10

Outsourcing and Automating Tasks for Efficiency

In the world of affiliate marketing, time is money. The more time you can spend on revenue-generating activities, the more money you will make. Outsourcing and automating tasks can help you free up your time so that you can focus on the most important aspects of your business. By identifying the tasks that are consuming too much of your time, you can begin to delegate them to others or automate them using technology.

Outsourcing can be a great option for tasks that are outside of your expertise or are taking up too much of your time. This can include tasks such as content creation, social media management, email marketing, customer service, and more. By hiring a virtual assistant or outsourcing to a specialized company, you can free up your time and ensure that these tasks are still being completed at a high level.

Automation can also be a powerful tool in affiliate marketing. There are a variety of tools and software available that can automate tasks such as email marketing, social media posting, lead generation, and more. By setting up these automated systems, you can streamline your workflow and ensure that important tasks are being completed consistently without taking up too much of your time.

It's important to note that while outsourcing and automation can be great time-savers, they do come with a cost. When outsourcing, you'll need to pay for the services you receive, and when automating, you'll need to pay for the tools and software you use. However, these costs can often be outweighed by the benefits of increased efficiency and more time to focus on revenue-generating activities.

When considering outsourcing or automation, it's important to carefully evaluate which tasks are most suitable for these solutions. You'll also need to research and compare different providers and tools to find the best fit for your needs and budget. It's also important to maintain communication and oversight of outsourced tasks to ensure that they are being completed to your satisfaction.

In summary, outsourcing and automating tasks can be powerful tools in affiliate marketing for increasing efficiency and freeing up time to focus on revenue-generating activities. However, it's important to carefully evaluate which tasks are most suitable for outsourcing or automation and to research and compare different providers and tools to find the best fit for your needs and budget. With these tools at your disposal, you can take your affiliate marketing business to the next level.

Chapter 10

Building Your Own Affiliate Program

If you've been successful in affiliate marketing, you may have considered building your own affiliate program. An affiliate program is a way for other marketers and content creators to promote your products or services and earn a commission for any resulting sales. By building your own affiliate program, you can leverage the power of other people's audiences to drive sales and grow your business.

Before you dive into building your own affiliate program, there are a few things you should consider. First, you'll need to determine your commission structure. How much will you pay affiliates for each sale? Will you offer a flat rate or a percentage of the sale? Next, you'll need to determine what marketing materials you'll provide to affiliates. This might include banner ads, email templates, and social media posts.

Once you have a plan in place, it's time to start building your affiliate program. Here are some steps to get started:

1. Choose an Affiliate Management Platform: There are several affiliate management platforms available that can help you manage your affiliate program. Some popular options include ShareASale, ClickBank, and Commission Junction. Look for a platform that offers the features you need, such as real-time tracking, automated payments, and detailed reporting.
2. Create a Sign-Up Page: You'll need a dedicated sign-up page where potential affiliates can learn more about your program and sign up to participate. This page should include information about your commission structure, marketing materials, and any requirements for joining.
3. Provide Marketing Materials: As mentioned earlier, you'll need to provide marketing materials to your affiliates. This might include banner ads, email templates, and social media posts. Make it easy for your affiliates to access and use these materials by providing

them with a centralized location where they can download what they need.
4. Set Up Tracking: You'll need to track your affiliates' sales to ensure that you're paying commissions accurately. Your affiliate management platform should provide real-time tracking and reporting, so you can keep an eye on sales and payouts.
5. Promote Your Program: Once your affiliate program is up and running, it's time to start promoting it. Reach out to your existing network of contacts and let them know about your program. You can also advertise your program on social media, blogs, and other online channels to attract new affiliates.
6. Monitor and Optimize: Finally, it's important to monitor your program's performance and adjust as needed. Use the reporting tools provided by your affiliate management platform to track sales, commissions, and other metrics. Look for areas where you can improve your program, such as by offering higher commissions or creating new marketing materials.

Building your own affiliate program can be a great way to expand your business and increase your profits. By creating a program that offers attractive commissions, providing your affiliates with the necessary tools and resources, and effectively managing your program, you can attract high-quality affiliates who will promote your products and services to a wider audience. Remember to continually evaluate and improve your program to ensure its success. With dedication and effort, you can build a thriving affiliate program that supports the growth and success of your business.

Chapter 11: Overcoming Challenges in Affiliate Marketing

Chapter 11

Common Challenges Faced by Affiliate Marketers

Affiliate marketing can be a lucrative way to make passive income online, but it's not without its challenges. In this section, we'll look at some of the common obstacles faced by affiliate marketers and how to overcome them.

One of the biggest challenges an affiliate marketer faces is competition. With so many people trying to make money online, it can be difficult to stand out from the crowd. To combat this, it's important to find a niche and build a loyal audience.

Another challenge is staying up to date with the latest marketing strategies and trends. With technology evolving at a rapid pace, it can be hard to keep up. To overcome this, it's important to continually educate yourself and stay informed about new techniques and platforms.

Getting traffic to your site can also be a challenge. Without traffic, you won't have anyone to promote your affiliate products to. To increase traffic, you can use strategies such as SEO, social media marketing, and paid advertising.

Another challenge is finding the right affiliate products to promote. It's important to choose products that are relevant to your audience and have a high conversion rate. To find the right products, you can use affiliate networks and conduct thorough research.

Tracking and analyzing data is also essential to success in affiliate marketing. Without accurate data, it's hard to know what's working and what's not. To overcome this challenge, use tracking tools and regularly analyze your data to make informed decisions.

Building trust with your audience can also be a challenge. People are becoming increasingly skeptical of online marketing, and it can take time to build trust with your audience. To overcome this, provide value to your audience and be transparent about your affiliations.

Finally, affiliate marketers may face challenges with payment processing and receiving commissions. It's important to choose reputable affiliate programs that offer reliable payment options and clear terms and conditions.

By being aware of these common challenges and developing strategies to overcome them, you can increase your chances of success as an affiliate marketer. Remember to stay focused, stay informed, and stay persistent in your efforts to build a profitable affiliate marketing business.

Chapter 11

How to Overcome These Challenges & Succeed in Affiliate Marketing

Affiliate marketing can be a profitable and exciting way to make passive income online. However, like any business venture, it comes with its own set of challenges. In this section, we will discuss some common challenges faced by affiliate marketers and provide tips on how to overcome them.

One of the biggest challenges faced by affiliate marketers is finding the right niche and products to promote. With so many options available, it can be overwhelming to choose the right ones. To overcome this challenge, take the time to research different niches and products to find ones that align with your interests and values. This will make it easier to promote them authentically and with enthusiasm.

Another challenge is driving traffic to your affiliate links. Without traffic, you won't make any sales. To overcome this, focus on building a strong online presence through social media, email marketing, and SEO. Additionally, consider investing in paid advertising to drive targeted traffic to your affiliate links.

A common challenge for affiliate marketers is building trust with their audience. People are bombarded with ads every day, and it can be hard to stand out and build a relationship with potential customers. To overcome this, focus on providing value to your audience through helpful content and honest product reviews. This will build trust and credibility, making it more likely that people will buy from your affiliate links.

Another challenge is keeping up with the latest trends and changes in the affiliate marketing industry. To overcome this, stay informed by reading industry blogs and attending webinars and conferences. Networking with other affiliate marketers can also help you stay up to date on industry developments.

One challenge that many affiliate marketers face is dealing with low conversion rates. It can be discouraging to put in a lot of effort and not see the results you want. To overcome this, focus on optimizing your sales funnel and improving your copywriting skills. A/B testing different landing pages and offers can also help improve your conversion rates.

A challenge that is often overlooked but important to address is the need to maintain a healthy work-life balance. Affiliate marketing can be time-consuming and stressful, which can lead to burnout. To overcome this, prioritize self-care and set boundaries around your work schedule. Make time for hobbies and activities outside of work to help you recharge and stay motivated.

Lastly, dealing with affiliate program and platform issues can be a challenge. This could include issues such as delayed payments, changes to commission rates, or technical problems with tracking. To overcome this, choose reputable affiliate programs and platforms, and regularly check your earnings and analytics to ensure everything is running smoothly.

Affiliate marketing comes with its own set of challenges, but with the right mindset and strategies, they can be overcome. Focus on providing value to your audience, staying informed on industry developments, optimizing your sales funnel, and taking care of yourself to ensure long-term success in the field. Remember that success in affiliate marketing requires patience, persistence, and a willingness to adapt to change.

Chapter 11

Tips and Strategies for Long-Term Success

Affiliate marketing can be a lucrative way to generate passive income online, but it requires dedication, hard work, and a long-term perspective. In this section, we'll explore some key tips and strategies for building a sustainable and profitable affiliate marketing business. Whether you're a beginner or an experienced affiliate marketer, these insights will help you stay ahead of the curve and achieve your goals.

1. Build Trust with Your Audience: One of the most important things you can do is build trust with your audience. This means being transparent, honest, and providing valuable information. People are more likely to buy from someone they trust, so it's important to establish that trust early on.
2. Choose the Right Products: It's important to choose products that are a good fit for your audience. Make sure you understand their needs and preferences before recommending products. It's also a good idea to choose products that offer good commissions and have a good reputation.
3. Diversify Your Income: Don't rely on just one affiliate program or product. Diversify your income by promoting multiple products or programs. This will not only increase your earning potential but also reduce your risk if one program or product stops performing well.
4. Stay Up to Date on Industry Trends: Affiliate marketing is constantly evolving, so it's important to stay up-to-date on industry trends. This includes changes in consumer behavior, new products and programs, and changes in advertising policies.
5. Build Relationships with Other Affiliate Marketers: Building relationships with other affiliate marketers can be beneficial for a number of reasons. You can learn from their experiences, collaborate on promotions, and share tips and strategies.
6. Focus on Content: Content is king in affiliate marketing. Create high-quality content that provides value to your audience. This can include blog posts, videos, social media posts, and more. Make sure

your content is optimized for search engines and shareable on social media.
7. Use Data to Optimize Your Strategy: Use data to track your progress and optimize your strategy. This includes tracking your traffic, clicks, and conversions. Use this information to make informed decisions about which products to promote and which marketing strategies to use.
8. Be Patient: Affiliate marketing is not a get-rich-quick scheme. It takes time to build a successful business. Be patient, persistent, and focus on building a long-term strategy for success.
9. Continuously Learn and Improve: Finally, continuously learn and improve your skills. Attend industry events, read blogs and books, and take courses to stay current on the latest trends and best practices.

By following these tips and strategies, you can build a successful affiliate marketing business that generates passive income for years to come. Remember, it takes time and effort, but with patience and persistence, you can achieve long-term success in this exciting and rewarding industry.

Chapter 12: Staying Informed of the Latest Affiliate Marketing Trends

Chapter 12

Understanding the Latest Affiliate Marketing Trends

Affiliate marketing is a constantly evolving industry, with new trends and changes emerging all the time. It's important for affiliate marketers to stay informed of the latest trends and best practices in order to stay ahead of the competition and continue to grow their business. In this section, we will discuss some of the most important trends and changes that are currently affecting the affiliate marketing industry.

One of the biggest trends in affiliate marketing right now is the rise of influencer marketing. Influencer marketing involves partnering with social media influencers and bloggers to promote products and services to their followers. This type of marketing can be extremely effective, as influencers often have a loyal and engaged following that trusts their recommendations. Affiliate marketers can take advantage of this trend by partnering with relevant influencers in their niche and offering them commission for any sales that result from their promotions.

Another important trend in affiliate marketing is the increasing use of video content. Videos are becoming an increasingly popular form of content across all social media platforms, and affiliate marketers are taking notice. By creating engaging and informative videos that showcase products or services, affiliates can attract new customers and increase their conversions.

Mobile optimization is another trend that is becoming increasingly important for affiliate marketers. As more and more people use their mobile devices to browse the internet and make purchases, it's essential for affiliate marketers to ensure that their websites and landing pages are fully optimized for mobile users. This means ensuring that pages load quickly, are easy to navigate, and are designed with mobile users in mind.

Another trend that is impacting the affiliate marketing industry is the rise of voice search. With the growing popularity of virtual assistants like Siri and Alexa, more and more people are using voice search to find information and make purchases online. Affiliate marketers can take advantage of this trend by ensuring that their content is optimized for voice search, using natural language and long-tail keywords.

Finally, privacy and data protection are becoming increasingly important concerns for consumers. With the introduction of regulations like GDPR and CCPA, consumers are more aware of their data privacy rights and are increasingly concerned about how their data is being used by companies. Affiliate marketers can address this trend by being transparent about their data collection practices and ensuring that they are fully compliant with all relevant regulations.

Understanding the latest affiliate marketing trends is essential for any affiliate marketer looking to stay ahead of the curve and grow their business. By keeping up with the latest trends in influencer marketing, video content, mobile optimization, voice search, and data privacy, affiliate marketers can ensure that they are providing the best possible experience for their customers and maximizing their earning potential.

Chapter 12

Staying Ahead of the Curve in Affiliate Marketing

In the ever-evolving world of affiliate marketing, it is crucial to stay ahead of the curve to maintain success and profitability. This means keeping up with the latest trends, technologies, and best practices in the industry. Here are some tips for staying ahead of the curve in affiliate marketing:

1. Affiliate marketing blogs: There are many affiliate marketing blogs out there that provide updates on the latest trends and news in the industry. Some popular blogs include Affiliate Marketing Blog by Geno Prussakov, Affiliate Tip by Shawn Collins, and Affiliaxe's Blog.
2. Industry publications: Industry publications such as PerformanceIN, Affiliate Summit, and Marketing Dive often provide in-depth coverage of the latest affiliate marketing trends, news, and developments.
3. Social media: Following industry leaders and influencers on social media platforms such as Twitter and LinkedIn can provide valuable insights into the latest trends and news in affiliate marketing.
4. Affiliate networks: Affiliate networks such as ShareASale, Commission Junction, and Awin often provide newsletters and updates on the latest trends and developments in the industry.
5. Webinars and events: Attending webinars and industry events such as Affiliate Summit, Affiliate World, and CJU can provide insights into the latest affiliate marketing trends and allow you to connect with other professionals in the industry.
6. Google Trends: Google Trends is a free tool that allows you to track search trends and see what topics are currently popular. This can be useful for identifying emerging trends in affiliate marketing.
7. Analytics tools: Analytics tools such as Google Analytics and Hotjar can provide insights into user behavior and help you identify trends in your own affiliate marketing campaigns.

There are many great resources on YouTube and podcasts that can help affiliate marketers stay ahead of the curve. These resources can be a great way for novice affiliate marketers to stay up to date with the latest trends and strategies in the industry. Here are a few recommendations:

1. Affiliate Marketing Mastery: This YouTube channel run by Stefan James covers a wide range of affiliate marketing topics, including the latest trends and strategies.
2. Affiliate Buzz: Hosted by James Martell, this podcast features interviews with top affiliate marketers and covers the latest industry news and trends.
3. Niche Pursuits: This YouTube channel and podcast hosted by Spencer Haws focuses on building successful niche websites and includes discussions on affiliate marketing trends and strategies.
4. Smart Passive Income: Hosted by Pat Flynn, this podcast covers a wide range of topics related to online business, including affiliate marketing trends and strategies.
5. CharlesNgo.com: This YouTube channel and blog run by Charles Ngo provides valuable insights and strategies for affiliate marketers, including the latest trends and best practices.

Staying ahead of the curve in affiliate marketing requires a willingness to learn, experiment, and adapt to new trends and technologies. By staying curious, open-minded, and customer-focused, you can maintain success and profitability in this dynamic and exciting industry.

Chapter 12

Using New Strategies and Technologies to Improve Your Affiliate Marketing

In today's fast-paced digital world, keeping up with the latest strategies and technologies is key to success in affiliate marketing. As a novice affiliate marketer, it's important to explore and experiment with new tools and techniques to enhance your marketing efforts and boost your revenue. In this section, we will discuss some of the latest and most effective strategies and technologies to improve your affiliate marketing.

One of the newest and most effective strategies in affiliate marketing is influencer marketing. This involves partnering with social media influencers who have a large following and can promote your product to their audience. Influencers can be bloggers, YouTubers, Instagrammers, or any other type of social media influencer. By partnering with an influencer, you can tap into their audience and benefit from their credibility and trustworthiness.

Another effective strategy is retargeting, which involves showing ads to people who have previously interacted with your brand or website. This can be done using pixels and cookies to track users and display targeted ads to them across various platforms. Retargeting is a powerful way to reach potential customers who have already shown interest in your brand and can result in higher conversion rates.

Automation is another area where new technologies are making a big impact. Marketing automation tools can help streamline your marketing efforts, allowing you to focus on creating content and building relationships with your audience. With automation, you can set up email campaigns, social media posts, and other marketing tasks to run on autopilot, freeing up your time to focus on other aspects of your business.

Artificial intelligence is another technology that is revolutionizing affiliate marketing. AI can be used to optimize ad campaigns, analyze data, and provide insights into customer behavior. Machine learning algorithms can help predict which products are most likely to convert and adjust your marketing efforts accordingly. There are various AI resources that can be used to improve affiliate marketing efforts, including:

1. AI-powered chatbots: Chatbots can be used to improve customer service, increase engagement, and enhance user experience.
2. AI-powered personalization: Personalization can be achieved using AI to create customized experiences for customers, such as personalized recommendations, content, and offers.
3. AI-powered analytics: AI-powered analytics can help analyze large amounts of data to provide insights into customer behavior, trends, and preferences. This information can be used to optimize marketing campaigns and improve ROI.
4. AI-powered content creation: AI can be used to create content, such as product descriptions, social media posts, and email marketing messages.
5. AI-powered ad targeting: AI can be used to target ads to specific audiences based on their interests, demographics, and behavior.

Some AI tools and resources that can be used for affiliate marketing include Google AdSense, Google Analytics, IBM Watson, Hootsuite Insights, and SalesForce Einstein. These tools can help with keyword research, data analysis, personalization, and automation. It's important to note that while AI can be a powerful tool for affiliate marketing, it should not be relied on entirely. A human touch is still needed to create meaningful content and engage with customers.

Affiliate marketing is constantly evolving, and it's important to stay ahead of the curve to succeed in this competitive industry. By using new strategies and technologies, you can improve your marketing efforts and increase your revenue. Experimenting with new tools and techniques, following industry trends, and staying current with the latest developments will help you stay ahead of the competition and succeed in affiliate marketing.

Chapter 13: Legal & Ethical Considerations in Affiliate Marketing

Chapter 13

Understanding the Legal and Ethical Issues in Affiliate Marketing

Affiliate marketing has the potential to be a lucrative and rewarding way to earn passive income, but it is important for novice affiliate marketers to understand the legal and ethical issues that come with it. As with any type of marketing, there are rules and regulations that govern the industry, and violating these rules can result in serious consequences. In this section, we will explore the legal and ethical issues in affiliate marketing and provide tips on how to navigate them.

First and foremost, it is important to understand that affiliate marketing is subject to the same laws and regulations as any other type of marketing. This includes laws related to advertising, consumer protection, and data privacy. For example, in the United States, the Federal Trade Commission (FTC) has guidelines that require affiliate marketers to disclose their relationship with the advertiser and any compensation they receive for promoting a product or service.

In addition to legal considerations, there are also ethical issues to consider in affiliate marketing. For example, it is important to promote products and services that you truly believe in and that are of value to your audience. Promoting low-quality products or products that are irrelevant to your audience can damage your reputation and lead to a loss of trust from your followers.

Another ethical consideration is the use of fake reviews or testimonials. It is never acceptable to fabricate positive reviews or testimonials in order to promote a product. Not only is this unethical, it is also illegal in many jurisdictions.

Transparency is key when it comes to ethical affiliate marketing. Disclosing your relationship with the advertiser and any compensation you receive for promoting a product is not only required by law, it is also an ethical responsibility. This transparency builds trust with your audience and ensures that they understand the nature of the relationship between you and the advertiser.

Another important ethical consideration in affiliate marketing is the use of data. Collecting data on your audience can be a valuable way to improve your marketing efforts, but it is important to do so ethically and transparently. This means being clear about what data you are collecting and how you plan to use it, and giving your audience the ability to opt out of data collection if they choose.

In addition to legal and ethical considerations, there are also practical considerations to keep in mind when it comes to affiliate marketing. For example, it is important to choose affiliate programs and products that align with your brand and audience. This will help ensure that you are promoting products that are relevant and valuable to your followers, and that you maintain your credibility as an influencer.

It is also important to be selective about the affiliate programs and products that you promote. Choosing too many affiliate programs or promoting too many products can dilute your message and make it difficult for your audience to distinguish between sponsored content and genuine recommendations. It is better to focus on a few high-quality affiliate programs and products that truly align with your brand and audience.

Finally, it is important to keep yourself informed on the latest legal and ethical issues in affiliate marketing. The industry is constantly evolving, and staying informed is key to avoiding legal and ethical pitfalls. This may include reading industry publications, attending conferences or webinars, and networking with other affiliate marketers to share best practices and insights.

Affiliate marketing can be a lucrative and rewarding way to earn passive income, but it is important to approach it with a strong understanding of the legal and ethical issues involved. By being transparent, ethical, and selective in your affiliate marketing efforts, you can build a successful and sustainable business that is both profitable and reputable.

Chapter 13

Complying with FTC Regulations

Affiliate marketers must always be aware of the legal and ethical issues involved in their work. One of the most important regulatory bodies that affiliate marketers must comply with is the Federal Trade Commission (FTC), which sets the guidelines for advertising in the United States. The FTC requires all affiliate marketers to disclose their relationship with the advertiser and to provide clear and conspicuous disclosures to consumers.

The first step in complying with FTC regulations is to understand the guidelines set forth by the agency. The FTC guidelines require that affiliate marketers clearly disclose their relationship with the advertiser, and this disclosure must be made clearly and conspicuous to consumers. This means that the disclosure must be easily seen and understood by consumers, and it must be placed in a location that is likely to be seen by consumers.

In addition to disclosure requirements, the FTC also requires that affiliate marketers avoid making false or misleading claims about the products or services they are promoting. Affiliate marketers must be honest and transparent in their advertising, and they must ensure that their claims are backed up by reliable evidence. If an affiliate marketer is found to be in violation of these guidelines, they may be subject to fines and other penalties.

To comply with FTC regulations, affiliate marketers should use clear and concise language in their disclosures. They should avoid using vague or ambiguous language that may confuse consumers. For example, an affiliate marketer may include a disclosure that states, "This post contains affiliate links," or "I may receive a commission if you make a purchase through my links."

Another way to comply with FTC regulations is to use tools and technologies that can help ensure compliance. For example, some affiliate marketing platforms offer built-in disclosure tools that can automatically add disclosures to affiliate links. These tools can help ensure that disclosures are made in a consistent and clear manner, which can help prevent confusion among consumers.

The FTC regularly updates its guidelines to reflect changes in the advertising landscape, and affiliate marketers must stay informed about these changes to ensure compliance. This can involve monitoring the FTC website and other industry resources to stay informed about any changes or updates to the guidelines.

Here are some key resources for complying with FTC regulations in affiliate marketing. By using these resources, affiliate marketers can ensure that they are complying with FTC regulations and maintaining ethical and transparent practices in their marketing efforts:

1. FTC Guides Concerning the Use of Endorsements and Testimonials in Advertising - This is the official document from the FTC that outlines the guidelines and requirements for using endorsements and testimonials in advertising. It covers topics such as disclosure, substantiation, and what constitutes deceptive practices.
2. FTC Endorsement Guides FAQ - This is a helpful resource that answers common questions about the FTC guidelines, including how to disclose material connections, how to handle sponsored content, and what the guidelines mean for social media influencers.
3. Copyblogger FTC Disclosure Examples - Copyblogger provides some examples of effective disclosure statements for different types of affiliate marketing content, such as product reviews, sponsored posts, and social media promotions.
4. Google AdSense Program Policies - If you are using Google AdSense to monetize your website or blog, it's important to comply with their program policies, which include requirements for disclosure of affiliate links and sponsored content.
5. Affiliate Marketing Compliance Checklist - This checklist from AvantLink covers all the key areas that affiliate marketers need to be aware of in order to comply with FTC regulations, including disclosure, content creation, and record-keeping.
6. Online Trust Alliance - The Online Trust Alliance provides guidance and best practices for compliance with privacy, security, and data protection laws, including the General Data Protection

Regulation (GDPR) in the EU and the California Consumer Privacy Act (CCPA) in the US. While these laws don't directly impact affiliate marketing, they do have implications for data collection and processing, which is an important consideration for many affiliate marketers.

Complying with FTC regulations is essential for affiliate marketers who want to build a successful and ethical business. By understanding the guidelines set forth by the FTC and using clear and concise language in their disclosures, affiliate marketers can help ensure compliance and avoid fines and other penalties. Using tools and technologies that can help ensure compliance and staying informed of the latest developments in FTC regulations can also help affiliate marketers stay ahead of the curve and build a successful and ethical affiliate marketing business.

Chapter 13

Protecting Your Reputation and Your Audience

As an affiliate marketer, it is important to understand that your reputation is everything. Your audience trusts you to provide them with accurate and honest information, and any breach of that trust can damage your reputation and hurt your business. It is important to take steps to protect your reputation and your audience. Here are some tips:

1. Be honest and transparent: Always disclose your affiliate relationships and be clear about any incentives you receive for promoting a product or service. This helps build trust with your audience and protects you from legal and ethical issues.
2. Only promote products or services you believe in: Don't promote products or services just for the sake of earning a commission. Make sure you believe in the product or service and that it is relevant to your audience.
3. Monitor your online presence: Keep an eye on what is being said about you online, including reviews and comments on social media. Respond to any negative feedback in a professional and courteous manner.
4. Protect your personal brand: Your personal brand is important to your success as an affiliate marketer. Make sure you are presenting yourself in a professional manner online and that your actions align with your brand values.
5. Be responsive to your audience: Respond promptly to any questions or concerns your audience may have. This helps build trust and credibility with your audience.
6. Stay up to date with industry news and trends: Keep yourself informed about any changes in your industry, including new products, services, or regulations. This helps you stay ahead of the curve and maintain your reputation as a trusted source of information.
7. Use proper marketing techniques: Follow ethical marketing practices, such as avoiding spam and deceptive advertising. This not

only protects your reputation but also ensures compliance with FTC regulations.
8. Consider the impact of your actions: Before making any decision related to your affiliate marketing business, consider how it may impact your reputation and your audience. Always act in a manner that aligns with your values and the best interests of your audience.
9. Build relationships with your audience: Take the time to build relationships with your audience through engagement on social media, email newsletters, and other channels. This helps build trust and loyalty and can help protect your reputation in the long run.

Protecting your reputation and your audience is critical to the success of your affiliate marketing business. By being honest, transparent, and ethical, and by staying up to date with industry trends and regulations, you can build a strong reputation as a trusted source of information and earn the trust and loyalty of your audience.

Chapter 14: Case Studies and Success Stories in Affiliate Marketing

Chapter 14

Learning from Other Successful Affiliate Marketers

Affiliate marketing can be a challenging field, and it's not always easy to know where to start or what strategies to use to achieve success. Fortunately, there are many successful affiliate marketers who are willing to share their knowledge and experience with others. In this section, we'll explore how learning from other successful affiliate marketers can help you grow your own affiliate marketing business.

One of the best ways to learn from successful affiliate marketers is to read their blogs, follow them on social media, and watch their videos. Many successful affiliate marketers share their insights and strategies through these channels, and by following them, you can gain valuable knowledge and inspiration. You can also learn from their mistakes and avoid making the same ones yourself.

Another great way to learn from successful affiliate marketers is to attend industry events and conferences. These events bring together some of the best and brightest minds in affiliate marketing, and they offer a great opportunity to network and learn from others. You can attend seminars and workshops led by successful affiliate marketers, and you can also meet with other affiliate marketers to exchange ideas and strategies.

You can also learn from successful affiliate marketers by joining online forums and groups. These forums and groups are a great place to ask questions, share ideas, and get feedback from others in the industry. You can connect with other affiliate marketers who are at the same level as you, as well as those who are more experienced and can offer guidance and advice.

Another way to learn from successful affiliate marketers is to partner with them on projects or campaigns. By working closely with successful affiliate marketers, you can gain valuable insights into their strategies and tactics, and you can also learn from their successes and failures. You can also leverage their expertise and reputation to help grow your own affiliate marketing business.

Finally, it's important to remember that learning from successful affiliate marketers is not just about copying what they do. It's important to develop your own unique voice and approach, and to find strategies that work best for you and your audience. By learning from others, you can gain inspiration and insight, but you should always put your own spin on things and strive to be innovative and original.

Here's a list of the Top 10 affiliate marketing blogs to enjoy as you dive deeper into the world of affiliate marketing:

1. Affiliate Tip - Affiliate Tip is a blog by Shawn Collins, who is a co-founder of the Affiliate Summit. The blog is full of tips and advice for affiliate marketers and is updated regularly.
2. Affiliate Marketing Blog by Geno Prussakov - Geno Prussakov is an affiliate marketing veteran and the founder of AM Navigator. His blog offers tips, news, and insights for affiliate marketers.
3. Missy Ward's Affiliate Marketing Blog - Missy Ward is an affiliate marketing veteran and the co-founder of Affiliate Summit. Her blog offers news, tips, and insights for affiliate marketers.
4. Charles Ngo's Affiliate Marketing Blog - Charles Ngo is a well-known affiliate marketer and his blog is a great resource for affiliate marketing tips and insights.
5. Affiliate Marketing Dude - Marcus Campbell is the Affiliate Marketing Dude and his blog offers tips and advice for affiliate marketers who are just starting out.
6. Zac Johnson's Affiliate Marketing Blog - Zac Johnson is a well-known affiliate marketer and his blog offers tips, news, and insights for affiliate marketers.
7. Finch Sells - Finch Sells is a blog by a well-known affiliate marketer who goes by the name Finch. His blog offers tips and advice for affiliate marketers who are looking to increase their earnings.
8. Affiliate Marketing School - Affiliate Marketing School is a blog by John Crestani, who is a well-known affiliate marketer. His blog offers tips, advice, and insights for affiliate marketers who are looking to succeed.

9. Affilorama - Affilorama is a blog and training platform for affiliate marketers. The blog offers tips, advice, and insights for affiliate marketers who are looking to succeed.
10. The Blogging Buddha - The Blogging Buddha is a blog by a well-known affiliate marketer who goes by the name Rae Dolan. Her blog offers tips and advice for affiliate marketers who are looking to succeed.

Here is a list of the top 10 affiliate marketing podcasts that provide excellent content and affiliate marketing information:

1. The Affiliate Guy Daily: Hosted by Matt McWilliams, this daily podcast covers a range of topics related to affiliate marketing, including how to find the right products to promote, building relationships with affiliate managers, and effective email marketing strategies.
2. Affiliate Buzz: This podcast is hosted by James Martell and Arlene Martell, who have been involved in affiliate marketing for over 20 years. They cover a range of topics related to affiliate marketing, including niche selection, content marketing, and affiliate program management.
3. Affiliate Marketing Mastery: Hosted by Stefan James, this podcast covers a range of topics related to affiliate marketing, including how to create and launch successful affiliate marketing campaigns, how to build a profitable email list, and how to create engaging content.
4. Niche Pursuits: Hosted by Spencer Haws, this podcast covers a range of topics related to affiliate marketing, including niche selection, keyword research, and content creation. The podcast also features interviews with successful affiliate marketers who share their insights and strategies.
5. The Smart Passive Income Podcast: Hosted by Pat Flynn, this podcast covers a range of topics related to building a successful online business, including affiliate marketing. The podcast features interviews with successful entrepreneurs and business owners, as well as practical tips and strategies for building a successful affiliate marketing business.

6. The Authority Hacker Podcast: Hosted by Gael Breton and Mark Webster, this podcast covers a range of topics related to building authority websites and affiliate marketing. The podcast features interviews with successful affiliate marketers, as well as practical tips and strategies for building a profitable affiliate marketing business.
7. The Blogging Millionaire: Hosted by Brandon Gaille, this podcast covers a range of topics related to building a successful blog, including affiliate marketing. The podcast features interviews with successful bloggers and online entrepreneurs, as well as practical tips and strategies for building a profitable affiliate marketing business.
8. Online Marketing Made Easy: Hosted by Amy Porterfield, this podcast covers a range of topics related to online marketing, including affiliate marketing. The podcast features interviews with successful entrepreneurs and business owners, as well as practical tips and strategies for building a successful affiliate marketing business.
9. Affilorama: Hosted by Mark Ling, this podcast covers a range of topics related to affiliate marketing, including niche selection, traffic generation, and content creation. The podcast also features interviews with successful affiliate marketers, as well as practical tips and strategies for building a profitable affiliate marketing business.
10. The Affiliate Insider Podcast: Hosted by Lee-Ann Johnstone, this podcast covers a range of topics related to affiliate marketing, including industry news, trends, and best practices. The podcast also features interviews with industry experts, as well as practical tips and strategies for building a successful affiliate marketing business.

Here are some of the Top 10 affiliate marketing YouTube channels for you to enjoy:

1. Pat Flynn - Pat Flynn is a successful affiliate marketer and entrepreneur who shares his insights and strategies on his YouTube channel. He provides step-by-step tutorials, case studies, and interviews with other successful marketers.

2. Miles Beckler - Miles Beckler is an online entrepreneur who focuses on affiliate marketing and content marketing. His channel provides in-depth tutorials, case studies, and step-by-step guides on building a successful affiliate marketing business.
3. Franklin Hatchett - Franklin Hatchett is an affiliate marketing expert who shares his strategies and tips for building successful affiliate marketing businesses. He covers a wide range of topics, from SEO to paid advertising.
4. Authority Hacker - Authority Hacker is a website that provides comprehensive guides and resources for building authority websites and profitable affiliate marketing businesses. Their YouTube channel features in-depth tutorials, case studies, and interviews with successful marketers.
5. Doug Cunnington - Doug Cunnington is an affiliate marketing expert who focuses on building niche websites and using SEO to drive traffic and sales. His channel provides in-depth tutorials and case studies on building successful affiliate marketing businesses.
6. Income School - Income School is a website and YouTube channel that provides comprehensive guides and resources for building niche websites and profitable affiliate marketing businesses. They offer a step-by-step approach to building and scaling affiliate marketing businesses.
7. Project Life Mastery - Project Life Mastery is a YouTube channel that provides a range of content on personal development, entrepreneurship, and affiliate marketing. Their affiliate marketing content includes in-depth tutorials, case studies, and interviews with successful marketers.
8. Coffeezilla - Coffeezilla is a YouTube channel that exposes scams and frauds in the online marketing world. They also provide in-depth reviews and analysis of various affiliate marketing programs and products.
9. John Crestani - John Crestani is a successful affiliate marketer and entrepreneur who provides in-depth tutorials, case studies, and interviews with other successful marketers. He covers a wide range of topics, from paid advertising to affiliate marketing strategies.

10. Odi Productions - Odi Productions is a YouTube channel that focuses on affiliate marketing and entrepreneurship. The channel provides tutorials, case studies, and interviews with successful affiliate marketers.

Learning from other successful affiliate marketers is a great way to grow your own affiliate marketing business. By reading their blogs, attending events, joining forums, partnering on projects, and developing your own unique approach, you can gain valuable knowledge and inspiration, and ultimately achieve long-term success in the field of affiliate marketing.

Chapter 14

Case Studies and Success Stories in Affiliate Marketing

Case studies and success stories are valuable resources for learning about the practical application of affiliate marketing strategies. In this section, we'll explore some real-world examples of successful affiliate marketing campaigns.

1. Amazon Associates - Amazon's affiliate program is one of the most well-known and successful programs in the industry. By promoting products on Amazon's platform, affiliates earn a commission on sales made through their unique affiliate links. Some of the keys to success for Amazon Associates include targeting specific niches, using high-quality product images, and regularly updating product links.
2. Pat Flynn - Pat Flynn is a successful affiliate marketer who has built a loyal following through his blog and podcast, Smart Passive Income. He's known for his transparency and willingness to share his successes and failures with his audience. Some of his most successful affiliate marketing campaigns have focused on promoting web hosting services and online courses.
3. Wirecutter - Wirecutter is a popular product review website that earns revenue through affiliate marketing. The site focuses on providing unbiased reviews of products across a range of categories, including technology, home and garden, and health and fitness. Wirecutter's success can be attributed to its dedication to thorough and impartial product testing, which has earned the site a reputation as a trusted source of information for consumers.
4. Skyscanner - Skyscanner is a travel comparison website that partners with airlines and other travel companies to offer users the best deals on flights, hotels, and rental cars. Affiliates earn a commission on bookings made through their unique referral links. Skyscanner's success is due in part to its user-friendly interface and its ability to provide users with customized travel recommendations based on their preferences and search history.

5. Making Sense of Cents - Making Sense of Cents is a personal finance blog that focuses on helping readers achieve financial independence through smart money management. The blog's founder, Michelle Schroeder-Gardner, has earned a reputation as a successful affiliate marketer by promoting products and services that align with her readers' interests and needs. Some of her most successful affiliate marketing campaigns have focused on promoting budgeting tools and investment platforms.
6. Food Blogger Pro - Food Blogger Pro is an online education platform that teaches aspiring food bloggers how to start and grow successful food blogs. The site's affiliate program allows bloggers to earn a commission on referrals to the platform. Food Blogger Pro's success is due in part to its focus on providing high-quality educational content and its dedication to building a community of supportive and engaged food bloggers.
7. Bluehost - Bluehost is a web hosting company that offers a popular affiliate program for bloggers and website owners. Affiliates earn a commission on sales made through their referral links. Bluehost's success can be attributed to its reputation as a reliable and affordable web hosting provider, as well as its dedication to providing excellent customer support.

There are several resources available online where you can learn more about successful case studies of affiliate marketing. These resources can provide valuable insights and inspiration for affiliate marketers looking to improve their strategies and achieve success in the industry. Here are a few options:

1. Affiliate Summit: Affiliate Summit is a website that offers resources and training for affiliate marketers. They also feature case studies on their website that highlight successful affiliate marketing campaigns.
2. Affiliate Marketing Dude: This is a website and YouTube channel run by Marcus Campbell, an experienced affiliate marketer. He shares case studies of his own successful campaigns as well as those of others in the industry.

3. Awin Blog: Awin is an affiliate marketing network that offers resources and support for affiliates. Their blog includes case studies that showcase successful campaigns and strategies used by affiliates.
4. Impact Blog: Impact is another affiliate marketing network that offers resources and support for affiliates. Their blog features case studies and success stories from both affiliates and advertisers.
5. NicheHacks: NicheHacks is a website that focuses on niche marketing and offers resources for affiliate marketers. They feature case studies and success stories from successful affiliates in various niches.

These case studies and success stories provide valuable insights into the strategies and tactics that successful affiliate marketers use to generate passive income online. By studying these examples, novice affiliate marketers can gain a better understanding of what it takes to succeed in the industry and develop their own successful campaigns.

Chapter 14

What You Can Learn from Their Strategies and Techniques

In the world of affiliate marketing, there are many successful marketers who have developed winning strategies and techniques to generate significant passive income online. As a novice in this field, it's essential to learn from their experiences and take advantage of their valuable insights. In this section, we will explore what you can learn from the strategies and techniques of successful affiliate marketers.

One of the most crucial things you can learn is how to choose the right products to promote. Successful affiliate marketers do extensive research on the products they promote, evaluating factors like their popularity, market demand, and commission rates. By choosing the right products, you can increase your chances of making significant profits.

Another important lesson is how to create engaging and valuable content that will attract your audience's attention. Successful affiliate marketers are skilled at crafting high-quality content that resonates with their audience, whether it's through blog posts, videos, social media, or email marketing. They also understand the importance of creating a strong personal brand to establish trust and credibility with their audience.

It's also essential to understand how to effectively use various marketing channels to reach your audience. Successful affiliate marketers use a range of marketing channels such as social media, search engine optimization, paid advertising, and email marketing to reach their audience and promote their products.

In addition, you can learn from successful affiliate marketers how to build and grow your email list. Building an email list is one of the most effective ways to generate passive income in affiliate marketing, as it allows you to establish a direct relationship with your audience and promote your products to them repeatedly over time.

Finally, successful affiliate marketers understand the importance of tracking and analyzing their results to optimize their strategies continually. They use tools like Google Analytics and other tracking software to monitor their website traffic, conversion rates, and other metrics to improve their performance and maximize their profits.

By studying the strategies and techniques of successful affiliate marketers, you can gain valuable insights into how to choose the right products, create engaging content, reach your audience effectively, build and grow your email list, and track and analyze your results. By applying these lessons to your own affiliate marketing efforts, you can increase your chances of success and generate significant passive income online.

Chapter 15: The Next Steps Are Yours

Chapter 15

Key Takeaways from this Book

Congratulations on making it through to the last few sections of "The Ultimate Guide to Affiliate Marketing"! By now, you should have a solid understanding of what affiliate marketing is, how it works, and how you can get started as an affiliate marketer.

Throughout this book, we've covered a lot of ground, from the basics of affiliate marketing to the latest trends and techniques. We've discussed how to find the right products and programs to promote, how to create content that resonates with your audience, and how to track and optimize your campaigns for maximum results.

So, what are the key takeaways from this book?

First and foremost, affiliate marketing is a viable and lucrative way to make money online. It's a low-risk, high-reward business model that allows you to earn passive income by promoting products and services you believe in.

To succeed in affiliate marketing, you need to focus on building trust and providing value to your audience. This means creating high-quality content that educates, entertains, and informs your readers. It also means being transparent about your affiliations and only promoting products that you genuinely believe in.

As we've discussed, there are many strategies and techniques you can use to improve your affiliate marketing campaigns, from SEO and social media marketing to email marketing and paid advertising. However, it's important to stay up to date with the latest trends and technologies and to always be testing and tweaking your campaigns for better results.

Finally, it's essential to stay ethical and compliant when it comes to affiliate marketing. This means following FTC guidelines, being transparent with your audience, and protecting your reputation, and your audience's trust always.

Affiliate marketing is a powerful and effective way to generate passive income online. By following the tips, strategies, and techniques outlined in this book, you can start building a successful affiliate marketing business today. So, what are you waiting for? Get started on your affiliate marketing journey and see how far it can take you! The next section will help you set your quest in motion.

Chapter 15

Putting Knowledge into Practice

Congratulations! You have made it to the end of "The Ultimate Guide to Affiliate Marketing." You have learned about the history of affiliate marketing, the benefits of affiliate marketing, the strategies for success, and the legal and ethical considerations.

Now it's time to put what you have learned into action. The following section will provide you with some practical tips on how to apply the knowledge you have gained.

First and foremost, establish a written copy of your plan. Pen to paper makes it feel more real. Set some goals for yourself and create a roadmap to achieve them. Identify your niche, your target audience, and the types of products or services you want to promote. Think about what makes you unique and what sets you apart from other affiliates.

Next, build your website or blog. Choose a domain name that is memorable and relevant to your niche. Create content that is engaging, informative, and valuable to your audience. Use search engine optimization (SEO) techniques to improve your website's visibility and attract more visitors.

Once your website is up and running, it's time to start promoting your affiliate products. You can do this through various channels, such as social media, email marketing, and paid advertising. Use analytics to track your results and adjust your strategies accordingly.

One of the keys to success in affiliate marketing is building relationships with your audience. Engage with your followers, answer their questions, and provide them with value beyond just promoting products. By doing so, you will build trust and loyalty with your audience, which can translate into increased sales.

Another important aspect of affiliate marketing is staying up to date with the latest trends and technologies. Continuously educate yourself on new marketing strategies, tools, and platforms. Attend conferences and webinars, read industry publications, and network with other affiliates.

Finally, don't forget about the legal and ethical considerations of affiliate marketing. Always disclose your affiliate relationship to your audience and comply with FTC regulations. Protect your reputation and the trust you have built with your audience by promoting only products that align with your values and meet your standards.

Affiliate marketing can be a lucrative and rewarding way to make passive income online. By following the strategies and techniques outlined in this guide, and by continuously learning and adapting, you can achieve long-term success in this exciting and dynamic industry.

Conclusion

Conclusion

Moving Forward with Your Affiliate Marketing Business

Congratulations on completing "The Ultimate Guide to Affiliate Marketing: How to Make Passive Income Online"! You now have a solid foundation of knowledge on affiliate marketing and the tools necessary to create a successful affiliate marketing business.

As you move forward with your affiliate marketing business, there are a few key things to keep in mind. First and foremost, remember that affiliate marketing is a long-term strategy, and success won't come overnight. It's important to be patient, persistent, and to continue learning and adapting as you go.

One of the best ways to continue learning is to keeping current on the latest trends, strategies, and technologies in the industry. Make a habit of regularly reading blogs, listening to podcasts, and watching videos from trusted sources. Stay connected with the affiliate marketing community through forums, social media groups, and networking events.

You should also make it a point to continually refine and optimize your strategies. Use data and analytics to track your progress and identify areas where you can improve. Experiment with different tactics, such as split testing different landing pages or trying out new traffic sources.

Staying organized and staying on top of your administrative tasks is critical to success. Keep track of your finances, including your earnings and expenses, and make sure you're complying with all relevant regulations and tax laws.

As your affiliate marketing business grows, you may want to consider building a team or outsourcing some of your tasks. This can help you scale your business and free up more time for other important tasks, such as creating content or building relationships with your audience.

Remember to stay focused on your goals and why you started your affiliate marketing business in the first place. Keep in mind the value you're providing to your audience and the potential for creating a sustainable passive income stream. With dedication, hard work, and a willingness to learn and adapt, you can build a successful affiliate marketing business that generates passive income for years to come.

As a final piece of advice, I would recommend that you stay persistent and patient in your affiliate marketing journey. Building a successful affiliate marketing business takes time, effort, and dedication. Success doesn't happen overnight, and it may take some time to see the results of your efforts. It's essential to stay focused on your goals, and consistently work towards them.

Don't be afraid to try new things and take calculated risks. The affiliate marketing industry is constantly evolving, and new opportunities may arise that can help you grow your business.

Lastly, always prioritize building strong relationships with your audience and affiliate partners. By focusing on providing value and building trust, you can create a loyal following and long-term partnerships that will benefit your business in the long run.

With the right mindset, strategies, and effort, you can achieve success in affiliate marketing and create a lucrative source of passive income online. Good Luck!

The Ultimate Guide to Affiliate Marketing: How to Make Passive Income Online

A Message from The Author

Dear Reader,

Thank you for taking the time to read *The Ultimate Guide to Affiliate Marketing: How to Make Passive Income Online*. I hope you found it informative and helpful in your own journey as an affiliate marketer.

As an author, the feedback I receive from readers like you is invaluable in helping me to continue to improve my writing and create content that is relevant and useful. That's why I would like to ask you to take a few minutes to leave a rating and review on the Amazon.

Not only does your review help me to know what I'm doing right and where I can improve, but it also helps other readers who are considering purchasing the book to make an informed decision. Your words have the power to influence others and to help them succeed in their own affiliate marketing ventures.

I would greatly appreciate your honest feedback, whether it's positive or negative. Your insights will not only help me to become a better writer, but they will also help other readers to benefit from the knowledge and experience that I've shared in this book.

Thank you again for your support and for taking the time to leave a review. It means the world to me.

Best regards,

Alex